Little Treasures

Sixteen Designs
by Lois Daykin
using Soft Baby.

Hannah

5

Harvey Swea
& Bruno H

Alexis

& *opposite*

Harvey

9

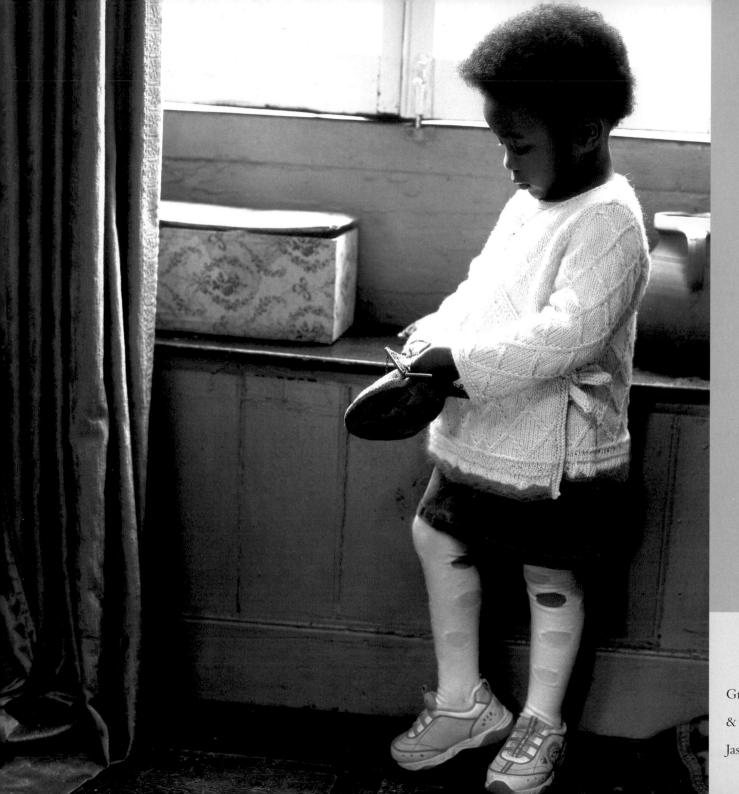

Grace

& opposite

Jasper

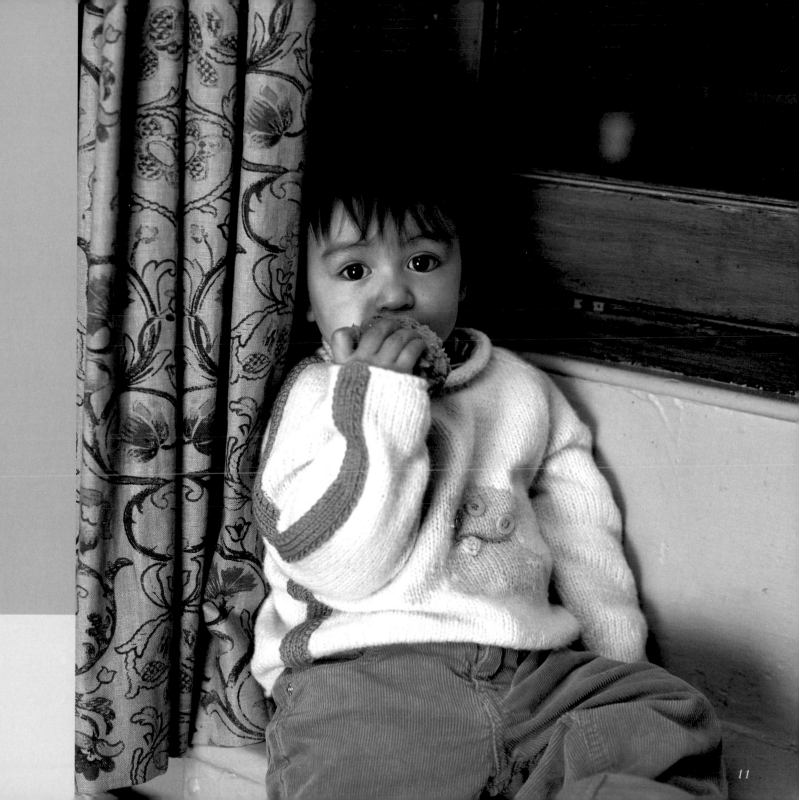

Odette

& *opposite*

Bea

Top Jasper Toy

left Agnes Toy

& *opposite* Agnes

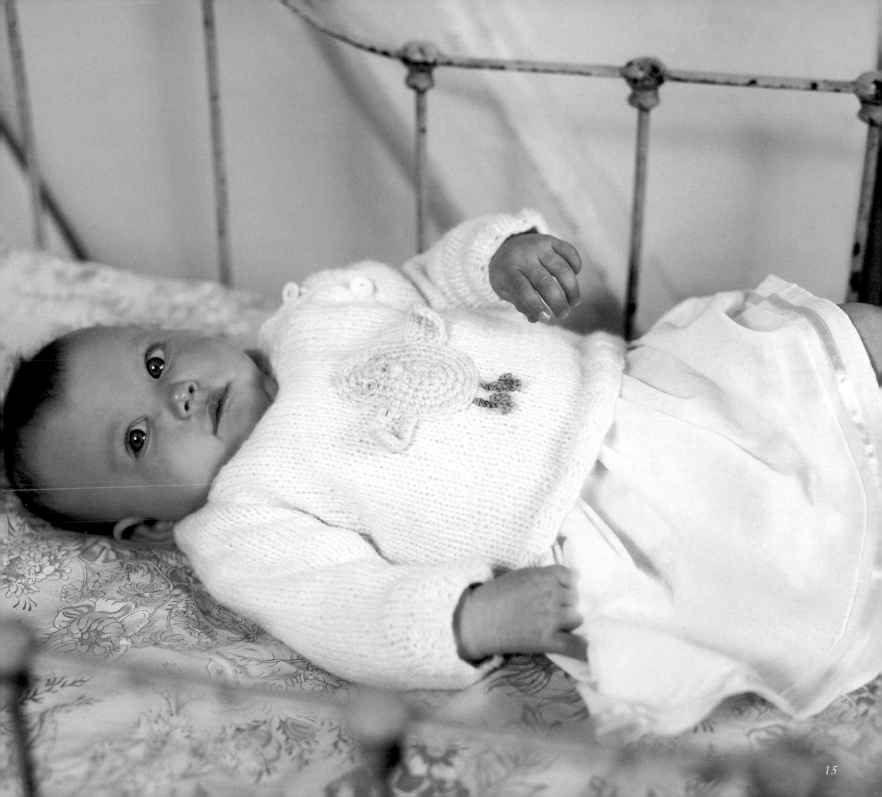

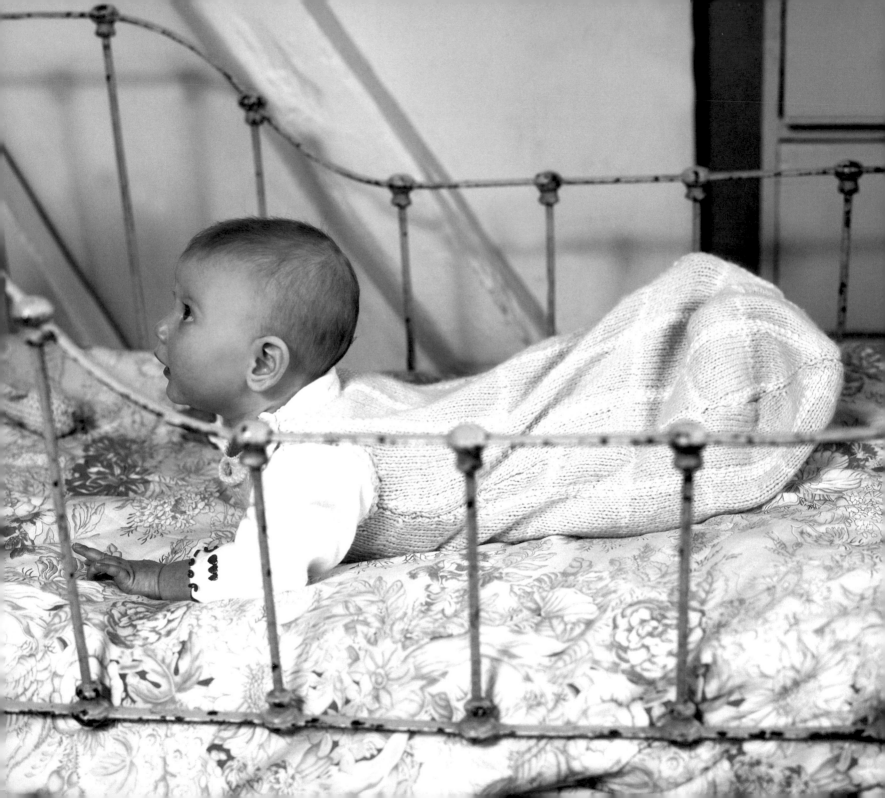

Agnes Hanging Cot Toy

& *opposite*

Odette Snuggle

17

Odette

Alexis

& *opposite*

Harvey

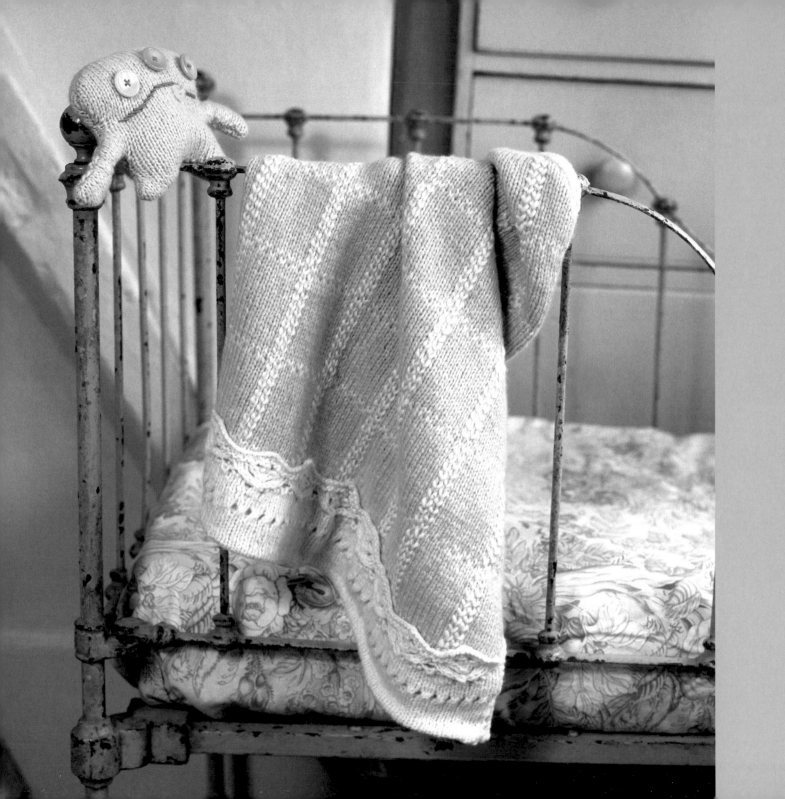

Jasper & Agnes Mobiles
& *opposite* Odette Blanket
& Jasper Toy

Madoc Cardigan

& opposite

Madoc Sweater

INDEX

ODETTE SNUGGLE

••

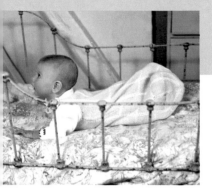

YARN

	3-6	6-12	months
To fit chest			
	46	51	cm
	18	20	in
Rowan Soft Baby			
A Princess 003			
	3	4	x50gm
B Cloud 001			
	1	2	x50gm

NEEDLES

1 pair 4mm (no 8) (US 6) needles
1 pair 4½mm (no 7) (US 7) needles

BUTTONS   2 x 00318

TENSION

20 sts and 28 rows to 10 cm measured over stocking stitch using 4½mm (US 7) needles.

BACK

Using 4½mm (US 7) needles and yarn A cast on 40 [46] sts.
Beg and ending rows as indicated, using the **fairisle** technique as described on the information page, working chart rows 1 to 28 once only and then repeating chart rows 29 to 48 throughout, cont in patt from chart, which is worked entirely in st st, as folls:
Work 1 row.
Inc 1 st at each end of next 12 rows, then on foll 8 alt rows. 80 [86] sts, taking inc sts into patt.
Cont in patt, shaping sides by dec 1 st at each end of 10th and every foll 8th row until 52 [58] sts rem.
Cont straight until back meas 54 [57] cm, ending with RS facing for next row.

Shape armholes

Keeping patt correct, cast off 3 sts at beg of next 2 rows. 46 [52] sts.
Dec 1 st at each end of next 3 rows, then on foll 3 [4] alt rows. 34 [38] sts.
Cont straight until armhole meas 9 [10] cm, ending with RS facing for next row.

Shape back neck

Next row (RS): K9 [10] and turn, leaving rem sts on a holder.
Work each side of neck separately.
Dec 1 st at neck edge of next 4 rows. 5 [6] sts.
Work 1 row, ending with RS facing for next row.
Place markers at both ends of last row – this is shoulder point.

Shape shoulder strap

Work 8 rows, ending with RS facing for next row.
Next row (RS): patt 2 sts, yfwd, work 2 tog, patt 1 [2] sts.
Work 1 row, ending with RS facing for next row.
Dec 1 st at each end of next 2 rows.
Cast off rem 1 [2] sts.
With RS facing, rejoin yarn(s) to rem sts, cast off centre 16 [18] sts, patt to end.
Complete to match first side, reversing shapings.

FRONT

Work as given for back until 12 rows less have been worked than on back to beg of back neck shaping, ending with RS facing for next row.

Shape front neck

Next row (RS): K9 [10] and turn, leaving rem sts on a holder.
Work each side of neck separately.
Dec 1 st at neck edge of next 3 rows, then on foll alt row. 5 [6] sts.
Work 6 rows, end with RS facing for next row.
Dec 1 st at each end of next 2 rows.
Cast off rem 1 [2] sts.
With RS facing, rejoin yarn(s) to rem sts, cast off centre 16 [18] sts, patt to end.
Complete to match first side, reversing shapings.

MAKING UP

Press as described on the information page.
Following chart, swiss darn vertical lines onto main sections.
Join side and base seams using back stitch, or mattress stitch if preferred.

Edging

Using 4mm (US 6) needles and yarn B cast on 2 sts.
Work in g st until edging, when slightly stretched, fits around entire armhole, strap and neck edges, beg and ending at top of one side seam and ensuring edging will lie flat around curved edges.
Cast off.
Slip stitch edging in place, joining cast-on and cast-off edges at underarm.
Fold shoulder straps over onto fronts level with shoulder markers and attach buttons to ends of front straps to correspond.

65 [69] cm (25.5 [27] in)

26 [29] cm 10 [11.5] in)

40 [43] cm 15.5 [17] in)

Key

☐ A - K on RS, P on WS

☐ B - K on RS, P on WS

⊡ swiss darn using B

Key   ☐ A   ☐ B   ⊡ Swiss darn using B

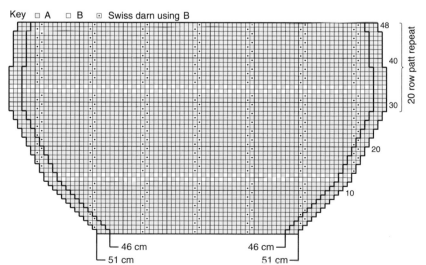

20 row patt repeat

46 cm
51 cm

46 cm
51 cm

GRACE

••

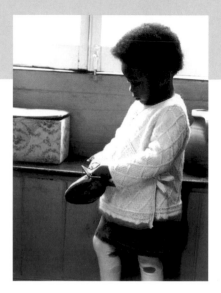

YARN

3-6	6-12					months
		1-2	2-3	3-4	4-5	years

To fit chest

46	51	56	58	61	64	cm
18	20	22	23	24	25	in

Rowan Soft Baby and Kidsilk Haze

A BabyPrinc.003

3	3	4	4	5	5	x 50gm

B KSHMajes.589

1	1	1	1	1	1	x 25gm

C KSHGrace 580

1	1	1	1	1	1	x 25gm

NEEDLES

1 pair 4mm (no 8) (US 6) needles
1 pair 4½mm (no 7) (US 7) needles
Cable needle

BUTTONS – 1 x 00321

TENSION

23 sts and 28 rows to 10 cm measured over pattern using 4½mm (US 7) needles and yarn A.

SPECIAL ABBREVIATIONS

C2B = slip next st onto cable needle and leave at back of work, K1, then K1 from cable needle; **C2F** = slip next st onto cable needle and leave at front of work, K1, then K1 from cable needle.

LEFT FRONT

Under frill
Using 4mm (US 6) needles and yarn B cast on 71 [71: 85: 85: 85: 99] sts.
Work in g st for 2 rows, ending with RS facing for next row.
Break off yarn B and join in yarn C.
Row 3 (RS): K1, *K2, yfwd, K3, K3tog, K3, yfwd, K3, rep from * to end.
Row 4: *P4, yrn, P2, P3tog, P2, yrn, P3, rep from * to last st, P1.
Row 5: K1, *K4, yfwd, K1, K3tog, K1, yfwd, K5, rep from * to end.
Row 6: *P6, yrn, P3tog, yrn, P5, rep from * to last st, P1.
Beg with a K row, work in st st for 4 rows, ending with RS facing for next row.
Break yarn and leave sts on a holder.
Upper frill
Work as given for under frill to end of row 6.
Do NOT break yarn.
Join frills
Holding WS of upper frill against RS of under frill, K tog first st of upper frill with first st of under frill, K tog rem sts of upper frill with rem sts of under frill in same way.
71 [71: 85: 85: 85: 99] sts.
Next row (WS): P4 [4: 6: 5: 5: 3], P2tog, (P3 [8: 3: 4: 7: 3], P2tog) 12 [6: 14: 12: 8: 18] times, P to end.
58 [64: 70: 72: 76: 80] sts.
Join in yarn A.
Using yarn A, work in g st for 2 rows.
Using yarn C and beg with a K row, work in st st for 3 rows, ending with WS facing for next row.
Break off yarn C and cont using yarn A only.
Purl 3 rows, ending with RS facing for next row.
Change to 4½mm (US 7) needles.
Beg and ending rows as indicated and repeating the 20 row patt repeat throughout, cont in patt from chart as folls:★★
Work 12 [18: 24: 28: 32: 34] rows, ending with RS facing for next row.
Shape front slope
Keeping patt correct, dec 1 st at end of next row and at same edge on foll 17 [17: 19: 19:

21: 21] rows, ending with RS facing for next row. 40 [46: 50: 52: 54: 58] sts. (Left front should meas 17 [19: 22: 23: 25: 26] cm.)
Shape armhole
Keeping patt correct, cast off 3 sts at beg and dec 1 st at end of next row.
36 [42: 46: 48: 50: 54] sts.
Dec 1 st at front slope edge of next row.
35 [41: 45: 47: 49: 53] sts.
Dec 1 st at armhole edge of next 3 [3: 5: 5: 5: 5] rows, then on foll 3 [4: 3: 3: 3: 4] alt rows **and at same time** dec 1 st at front slope edge on every row.
20 [23: 26: 28: 30: 31] sts.
Dec 1 st at front slope edge **only** on next 12 [14: 16: 14: 16: 16] rows, then on foll 0 [0: 0: 3: 2: 2] alt rows.
8 [9: 10: 11: 12: 13] sts.
Cont straight until armhole meas 11 [12: 13: 14: 14: 15] cm, ending with RS facing for next row.
Shape shoulder
Cast off 4 [4: 5: 5: 6: 6] sts at beg of next row.
Work 1 row.
Cast off rem 4 [5: 5: 6: 6: 7] sts.

RIGHT FRONT

Work as given for left front, reversing shapings.

BACK

Work as given for left front to ★★.
Cont straight until back matches fronts to beg of armhole shaping, ending with RS facing for next row.
Shape armholes
Keeping patt correct, cast off 3 sts at beg of next 2 rows.
52 [58: 64: 66: 70: 74] sts.
Dec 1 st at each end of next 3 [3: 5: 5: 5: 5] rows, then on foll 3 [4: 3: 3: 3: 4] alt rows.
40 [44: 48: 50: 54: 56] sts.
Cont straight until back matches fronts to beg of shoulder shaping, ending with RS facing for next row.
Shape shoulders and back neck
Next row (RS): Cast off 4 [4: 5: 5: 6: 6] sts, patt until there are 7 [8: 8: 9: 9: 10] sts on

right needle and turn, leaving rem sts on a holder.
Work each side of neck separately.
Cast off 3 sts at beg of next row.
Cast off rem 4 [5: 5: 6: 6: 7] sts.
With RS facing, rejoin yarn to rem sts, cast off centre 18 [20: 22: 22: 24: 24] sts, patt to end.
Complete to match first side, reversing shapings.

SLEEVES

Using 4mm (US 6) needles and yarn A cast on 40 [44: 44: 46: 46: 48] sts.
Work in g st for 4 rows, ending with RS facing for next row.
Change to 4½mm (US 7) needles.
Beg and ending rows as indicated, cont in patt from chart as folls:
Dec 1 st at each end of 7th [7th: 7th: 9th: 9th: 9th] row.
38 [42: 42: 44: 44: 46] sts.
Work 19 [21: 13: 7: 11: 11] rows, ending with RS facing for next row.
Inc 1 st at each end of next and every foll 8th [14th: 10th: 10th: 10th: 10th] row until there are 42 [46: 50: 54: 54: 58] sts, taking inc sts into patt.
Cont straight until sleeve meas 17 [20: 23: 25: 27: 30] cm, ending with RS facing for next row.
Shape top
Keeping patt correct, cast off 3 sts at beg of next 2 rows. 36 [40: 44: 48: 48: 52] sts.
Dec 1 st at each end of next 3 rows, then on foll 4 alt rows, then on every row until 12 sts rem, ending with RS facing for next row.
Cast off rem 12 sts.

MAKING UP

Press as described on the information page.
Join both shoulder seams using back stitch, or mattress stitch if preferred.
Side borders (both alike)
With RS facing, using 4mm (US 6) needles and yarn A, pick up and knit 21 [25: 29: 32: 34: 36] sts evenly along side edge of front, between cast-on edge of under frill and beg

of front slope shaping.

Work in g st for 2 rows, ending with WS facing for next row.

Cast off knitwise (on WS).

Neck border and right tie

Using 4mm (US 6) needles and yarn A, cast on 40 sts (for tie), then with RS facing and beg and ending at cast-off edges of side borders, pick up and knit 50 [54: 58: 62: 64: 66] sts up right front slope to shoulder, 24 [26: 28: 28: 30: 30] sts from back, then 50 [54: 58: 62: 64: 66] sts down left front slope. 164 [174: 184: 192: 198: 202] sts.

Row 1 (WS): K2tog, yfwd (to make a buttonhole), K to end.

Row 2: Knit.

Cast off knitwise (on WS).

Left tie

Using 4mm (US 6) needles and yarn A, cast on 40 sts.

Work in g st for 2 rows, ending with WS facing for next row.

Cast off knitwise (on WS).

See information page for finishing instructions, setting in sleeves using the set-in method.

Attach one end of left tie to left side seam, level with beg of front slope shaping. Attach button to inside of right side seam level with beg of front slope shaping.

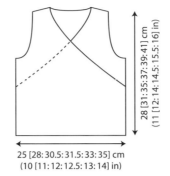

28 [31: 35: 37: 39: 41] cm
(11 [12: 14: 14.5: 15.5: 16] in)

25 [28: 30.5: 31.5: 33: 35] cm
(10 [11: 12: 12.5: 13: 14] in)

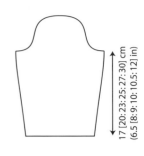

17 [20: 23: 25: 27: 30] cm
(6.5 [8: 9: 10: 10.5: 12] in)

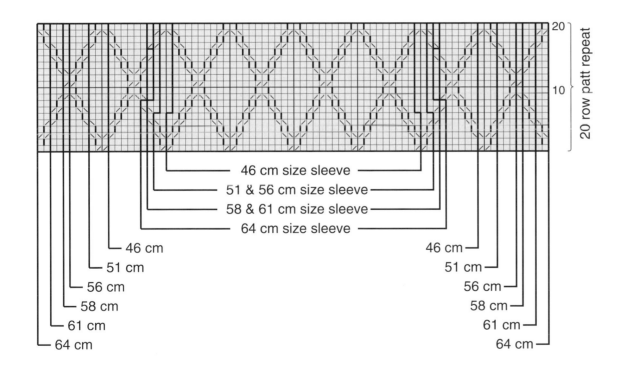

20 row patt repeat

46 cm size sleeve
51 & 56 cm size sleeve
58 & 61 cm size sleeve
64 cm size sleeve

46 cm
51 cm
56 cm
58 cm
61 cm
64 cm

46 cm
51 cm
56 cm
58 cm
61 cm
64 cm

Key

☐ K on RS,
   P on WS

▨ C2B

▧ C2F

HARVEY

••

YARN

| | 3-6 | 6-12 | | | | | months |
| | | | 1-2 | 2-3 | 3-4 | 4-5 | years |
| To fit chest |
| | 46 | 51 | 56 | 58 | 61 | 64 | cm |
| | 18 | 20 | 22 | 23 | 24 | 25 | in |
| **Rowan Soft Baby** |
| SweaterCosy 004 |
| | 3 | 3 | 4 | 4 | 5 | 5 | x50gm |
| SlipoverAngel 002 |
| | 2 | 2 | 3 | 3 | 3 | 4 | x50gm |

NEEDLES
1 pair 4mm (no 8) (US 6) needles
1 pair 4½mm (no 7) (US 7) needles
Cable needle

TENSION
24 sts and 30 rows to 10 cm measured over pattern using 4½mm (US 7) needles.

SPECIAL ABBREVIATIONS
C4B = slip next 2 sts onto cable needle and leave at back of work, K2, then K2 from cable needle; **C4F** = slip next 2 sts onto cable needle and leave at front of work, K2, then K2 from cable needle.

Sweater

BACK
Using 4mm (US 6) needles cast on 54 [58: 62: 66: 70: 70] sts.
Row 1 (RS): K2, *P2, K2, rep from * to end.
Row 2: P2, *K2, P2, rep from * to end.
These 2 rows form rib.
Work in rib for a further 3 [3: 5: 5: 5: 5] rows, ending with **WS** facing for next row.
Next row (WS): Rib 2 [1: 3: 1: 3: 1], inc in next st, (rib 6 [5: 4: 6: 6: 5], inc in next st) 7 [9: 11: 9: 9: 11] times, rib to end.
62 [68: 74: 76: 80: 82] sts.
Change to 4½mm (US 7) needles.
Row 1 (RS): Knit.
Row 2: P0 [3: 6: 7: 9: 10], *K2, P10, rep from * to last 2 [5: 8: 9: 11: 12] sts, K2, P0 [3: 6: 7: 9: 10].
Row 3: K0 [3: 2: 3: 5: 6], (C4F) 0 [0: 1: 1: 1: 1] times, *K2, C4B, K2, C4F, rep from * to last 2 [5: 8: 9: 11: 12] sts, (K2, C4B) 0 [0: 1: 1: 1: 1] times, K0 [3: 2: 3: 5: 6].
Row 4: As row 2.
These 4 rows form patt.
Cont in patt until back meas 17 [19: 22: 23: 25: 26] cm, ending with RS facing for next row.
Shape armholes
Keeping patt correct, cast off 3 sts at beg of next 2 rows. 56 [62: 68: 70: 74: 76] sts.**
Dec 1 st at each end of next 3 [5: 5: 5: 5: 5]

rows, then on foll 4 alt rows.
42 [44: 50: 52: 56: 58] sts.
Cont straight until armhole meas 11 [12: 13: 14: 14: 15] cm, ending with RS facing for next row.
Shape shoulders and back neck
Next row (RS): Cast off 4 [4: 5: 5: 6: 6] sts, patt until there are 7 [7: 8: 9: 9: 10] sts on right needle and turn, leaving rem sts on a holder.
Work each side of neck separately.
Cast off 3 sts at beg of next row.
Cast off rem 4 [4: 5: 6: 6: 7] sts.
With RS facing, rejoin yarn to rem sts, cast off centre 20 [22: 24: 24: 26: 26] sts, patt to end.
Complete to match first side, reversing shapings.

FRONT
Work as given for back to **.
Dec 1 st at each end of next 3 [4: 4: 4: 4: 4] rows. 50 [54: 60: 62: 66: 68] sts.
Work 1 [0: 0: 0: 0: 0] rows, ending with RS facing for next row.
Divide for neck
Next row (RS): K2tog, patt 21 [23: 26: 27: 29: 30] sts, K2tog and turn, leaving rem sts on a holder.
Work each side of neck separately.
Keeping patt correct, dec 1 [1: 1: 0: 1: 0] st at neck edge of next row.
22 [24: 27: 29: 30: 32] sts.
Dec 1 st at each end of next and foll 2 [3: 3: 3: 3: 3] alt rows. 16 [16: 19: 21: 22: 24] sts.
Dec 1 st at neck edge **only** on 2nd and foll 7 [7: 8: 9: 9: 9] alt rows, then on foll 0 [0: 0: 0: 0: 4th] row. 8 [8: 10: 11: 12: 13] sts.
Cont straight until front matches back to beg of shoulder shaping, ending with RS facing for next row.
Shape shoulder
Cast off 4 [4: 5: 5: 6: 6] sts at beg of next row.
Work 1 row.
Cast off rem 4 [4: 5: 6: 6: 7] sts.
With RS facing, rejoin yarn to rem sts, K2tog, patt to last 2 sts, K2tog.
Complete to match first side, reversing

shapings, working an extra row before beg of shoulder shaping.

SLEEVES
Using 4mm (US 6) needles cast on 30 [34: 34: 38: 38: 38] sts.
Work in rib as given for back for 5 [5: 7: 7: 7: 7] rows, ending with **WS** facing for next row.
Next row (WS): Rib 1 [1: 1: 3: 3: 1], inc in next st, (rib 3 [5: 5: 5: 5: 4], inc in next st) 7 [5: 5: 5: 5: 7] times, rib to end.
38 [40: 40: 44: 44: 46] sts.
Change to 4½mm (US 7) needles.
Row 1 (RS): Knit.
Row 2: P0 [1: 1: 3: 3: 4], *K2, P10, rep from * to last 2 [3: 3: 5: 5: 6] sts, K2, P0 [1: 1: 3: 3: 4].
Row 3: K0 [1: 1: 3: 3: 4], *K2, C4B, K2, C4F, rep from * to last 2 [3: 3: 5: 5: 6] sts, K2 [3: 3: 5: 5: 6].
Row 4: As row 2.
These 4 rows form patt.
Cont in patt, shaping sides by inc 1 st at each end of 7th [5th: 3rd: 3rd: 5th: 5th] and every foll 12th [12th: 8th: 8th: 10th: 10th] row to 44 [48: 50: 48: 54: 60] sts, then on every foll – [-: 10th: 10th: 12th: –] row until there are – [-: 52: 56: 56: –] sts, taking inc sts into patt.
Cont straight until sleeve meas 17 [20: 23: 25: 27: 30] cm, ending with RS facing for next row.
Shape top
Keeping patt correct, cast off 3 sts at beg of next 2 rows. 38 [42: 46: 50: 50: 54] sts.
Dec 1 st at each end of next 3 rows, then on foll 5 alt rows, then on foll 5 [7: 9: 11: 11: 13] rows, ending with RS facing for next row.
Cast off rem 12 sts.

POCKET
Using 4½mm (US 7) needles cast on 14 [14: 17: 17: 20: 20] sts.
Row 1 (RS): Knit.
Row 2: K2, P10, K2, P0 [0: 3: 3: 6: 6].
Row 3: (K2, C4F) 0 [0: 0: 0: 1: 1] times, K2 [2: 5: 5: 2: 2], C4B, K2, C4F, K2.
Row 4: As row 2.
These 4 rows form patt.
Cont in patt for a further 0 [0: 2: 2: 2: 2]

rows, ending with RS facing for next row.
Inc 1 st at beg of next and foll 3 alt rows,
then at same edge on foll 8 [8: 10: 10: 14: 14]
rows, taking inc sts into patt.
26 [26: 31: 31: 38: 38] sts.

3rd and 4th sizes
Next row (WS): Patt to last st, K1.
This row sets the sts – lower sts in patt with st
across upper edge of pocket worked as a K st
on every row.

All sizes
Cont as set for a further 21 [21: 24: 24: 25: 25]
rows, ending with RS facing for next row.
Dec 1 st at beg of next row and at same edge
on foll 8 [8: 10: 10: 14: 14] rows, then on foll
3 alt rows. 14 [14: 17: 17: 20: 20] sts.
Work a further 3 [3: 5: 5: 5: 5] rows, ending
with RS facing for next row.
Cast off in patt.

MAKING UP
Press as described on the information page.
Join right shoulder seam using back stitch, or
mattress stitch if preferred.
Neckband
With RS facing and using 4mm (US 6)
needles, pick up and knit 29 [33: 33: 37:
37: 41] sts down left side of neck, place
marker on needle, 29 [33: 33: 37: 37: 41] sts
up right side of neck, then 28 [28: 32: 32:

32: 32] sts from back.
86 [94: 98: 106: 106: 114] sts.
Beg with row 2, work in rib as given for back
for 1 row.
Row 2 (RS): Rib to within 2 sts of marker,
K2tog, slip marker to right needle, K2tog tbl,
rib to end.
Row 3: Rib to within 1 st of marker, P2
(marker is between these 2 sts), rib to end.
Rep last 2 rows once more, ending with RS
facing for next row.
82 [90: 94: 102: 102: 110] sts.
Cast off in rib, still decreasing either side of
marker as before.
Join left shoulder and neckband seam.
Pocket borders (both alike)
With RS facing and using 4mm (US 6)
needles, pick up and knit 20 [20: 24: 24:
28: 28] sts evenly along shaped row-end edge
of pocket opening.
Row 1 (WS): K1, *P2, K2, rep from * to last
3 sts, P2, K1.
Row 2: K3, *P2, K2, rep from * to last st, K1.
Row 3: As row 1.
Cast off in rib.
Using photograph as a guide, sew pocket onto
front.
See information page for finishing
instructions, setting in sleeves using the set-in
method.

Slipover

BACK, FRONT and POCKET
Work as given for sweater.

MAKING UP
Press as described on the information page.
Join right shoulder seam using back stitch, or
mattress stitch if preferred.
Neckband
Work as given for neckband of sweater.

Armhole borders (both alike)
With RS facing and using 4mm (US 6)
needles, pick up and knit 50 [54: 58: 62:
62: 66] sts evenly around armhole edge.
Beg with row 2, work in rib as given for back
for 3 rows.
Cast off in rib.
Pocket borders (both alike)
Work as given for pocket borders of sweater.
Using photo as a guide, sew pocket onto front.
See information page for finishing instructions.

26 [28.5: 31: 31.5: 33.5: 34] cm
(10 [11: 12: 12.5: 13: 13.5] in)

28 [31: 35: 37: 39: 41] cm
(11 [12: 14: 14.5: 15.5: 16] in)

17 [20: 23: 25: 27: 30] cm
(6.5 [8: 9: 10: 10.5: 12] in)

MADOC

••

YARN

	3-6	6-12					months
			1-2	2-3	3-4	4-5	years
To fit chest							
	46	51	56	58	61	64	cm
	18	20	22	23	24	25	in

Rowan Soft Baby and 4 ply Soft Sweater

A Baby Cosy 004

2	2	3	3	3	4	x50gm

B *4 ply Sooty 372

1	1	2	2	2	2	x50gm

C *4 ply Linseed 393

1	1	1	1	1	1	x50gm

D *4 ply Leafy 367

1	1	1	1	1	1	x50gm

Cardigan

A Baby Angel 002

3	3	3	4	4	5	x 50gm

B *4 ply Marine 380

1	1	1	1	1	2	x 50gm

C *4 ply Rain Cloud 387

1	1	1	1	1	1	x 50gm

D *4 ply Blue Bird 369

1	1	1	1	1	1	x 50gm

*Use 4 ply Soft DOUBLE throughout

NEEDLES
1 pair 4mm (no 8) (US 6) needles
1 pair 4½mm (no 7) (US 7) needles

BUTTONS – 1 for 1st and 2nd sizes of sweater, or 5 for cardigan

TENSION
20 sts and 28 rows to 10 cm measured over stocking stitch using 4½mm (US 7) needles and yarn A.

SPECIAL ABBREVIATIONS
ytf = yarn to front of work;
ytb = yarn to back of work.

Sweater

BACK
Using 4mm (US 6) needles and yarn B cast on 51 [57: 61: 63: 67: 69] sts.
Joining in and breaking off colours as required, cont in fancy rib as folls:
Row 1 (RS): Using yarn B K5 [4: 4: 5: 5: 4], (ytf, sl 1, ytb, K1) 0 [0: 0: 1: 1: 0: 1] times, *K2, ytf, sl 1, ytb, K1, rep from * to last 6 [5: 7: 4: 6: 7] sts, K6 [5: 2: 4: 6: 2], (ytf, sl 1, ytb, K4) 0 [0: 1: 0: 0: 1] times.
Row 2: Using yarn B P4, K1 [0: 2: 3: 1: 2], *ytf, sl 1, ytb, K3, rep from * to last 6 [5: 7: 4: 6: 7] sts, (ytf, sl 1, ytb) 1 [1: 1: 0: 1: 1] times,

K1 [0: 2: 0: 1: 2], P4.
Row 3: Using yarn B K4, using yarn A K0 [0: 0: 1: 0: 0], (ytf, sl 1, ytb) 0 [0: 1: 1: 0: 1] times, K1 [0: 1: 1: 1: 1], *K2, ytf, sl 1, ytb, K1, rep from * to last 6 [5: 7: 4: 6: 7] sts, K2 [1: 2: 0: 2: 2], (ytf, sl 1, ytb) 0 [0: 1: 0: 0: 1] times, using yarn B K4.
Row 4: Using yarn B P4, using yarn A K1 [0: 2: 3: 1: 2], *ytf, sl 1, ytb, K3, rep from * to last 6 [5: 7: 4: 6: 7] sts, (ytf, sl 1, ytb) 1 [1: 1: 0: 1: 1] times, K1 [0: 2: 0: 1: 2], using yarn B P4.
Row 5: Using yarn B K4, using yarn C K0 [0: 0: 1: 0: 0], (ytf, sl 1, ytb) 0 [0: 1: 1: 0: 1] times, K1 [0: 1: 1: 1: 1], *K2, ytf, sl 1, ytb, K1, rep from * to last 6 [5: 7: 4: 6: 7] sts, K2 [1: 2: 0: 2: 2], (ytf, sl 1, ytb) 0 [0: 1: 0: 0: 1] times, using yarn B K4.
Row 6: Using yarn B P4, using yarn C K1 [0: 2: 3: 1: 2], *ytf, sl 1, ytb, K3, rep from * to last 6 [5: 7: 4: 6: 7] sts, (ytf, sl 1, ytb) 1 [1: 1: 0: 1: 1] times, K1 [0: 2: 0: 1: 2], using yarn B P4.
Rows 7 and 8: As rows 3 and 4.
Row 9: Using yarn B K4, using yarn D K0 [0: 0: 1: 0: 0], (ytf, sl 1, ytb) 0 [0: 1: 1: 0: 1] times, K1 [0: 1: 1: 1: 1], *K2, ytf, sl 1, ytb, K1, rep from * to last 6 [5: 7: 4: 6: 7] sts, K2 [1: 2: 0: 2: 2], (ytf, sl 1, ytb) 0 [0: 1: 0: 0: 1] times, using yarn B K4.
Row 10: Using yarn B P4, using yarn D K1 [0: 2: 3: 1: 2], *ytf, sl 1, ytb, K3, rep from * to last 6 [5: 7: 4: 6: 7] sts, (ytf, sl 1, ytb) 1 [1: 1: 0: 1: 1] times, K1 [0: 2: 0: 1: 2], using yarn B P4.
Rows 11 and 12: As rows 3 and 4.
3rd, 4th, 5th and 6th sizes
Rows 13 to 16: As rows 1 to 4.
All sizes
Change to 4½mm (US 7) needles.
Break off yarn C and D and cont as folls:
Row 1 (RS): Using yarn B K4, using yarn A K to last 4 sts, using yarn B K4.
Row 2: Using yarn B P4, using yarn A P to last 4 sts, using yarn B P4.
These 2 rows form patt.
Cont in patt until back meas 15 [17: 21: 21: 23: 25] cm, ending with RS facing for next row.
Shape raglan armholes
Place markers at both ends of last row to denote base of armholes.

Next row (RS): Using yarn B K4, using yarn A sl 1, K1, psso, K to last 6 sts, K2tog, using yarn B K4.**
Working all raglan armhole decreases as set by last row, dec 1 st at each end of 4th and every foll 4th row to 43 [49: 53: 57: 61: 61] sts, then on every foll – [alt: alt: alt: alt: alt] row until – [45: 25: 25: 27: 27] sts rem.
Work 1 row, ending with RS facing for next row.
1st and 2nd sizes
Divide for back opening
Next row (RS): Using yarn B K4, using yarn A sl 1, K1, psso, K15 [16: -: -: -: -] and turn, leaving rem sts on a holder.
20 [21: -: -: -: -] sts.
Work each side of neck separately.
Next row (WS): Using yarn A K1, patt to end.
This row sets the sts – back opening edge st now in g st with all other sts still in st st.
Working all raglan armhole decreases as set, dec 1 st at raglan armhole edge of next and every foll alt row until 10 [11: -: -: -: -] sts rem.
Work 1 row, ending with RS facing for next row.
Break yarn and leave rem 10 [11: -: -: -: -] sts on a holder.
With RS facing, rejoin yarn to rem sts, K2tog, patt to last 6 sts, K2tog, using yarn B K4. 20 [21: -: -: -: -] sts.
Next row (WS): Patt to last st, using yarn A K1.
Complete to match first side, reversing shapings.
3rd, 4th, 5th and 6th sizes
Break yarn and leave rem – [-: 25: 25: 27: 27] sts on a holder.

FRONT
Work as given for back to **.
Working all raglan armhole decreases as set by last row, dec 1 st at each end of 4th and every foll 4th row to 43 [49: 53: 57: 61: 61] sts, then on every foll alt row until 37 [39: 43: 43: 45: 45] sts rem.
Work 1 row, ending with RS facing for next row.

32

Shape neck

Next row (RS): Using yarn B K4, using yarn A sl 1, K1, psso, K9 [9: 11: 11: 11: 11] and turn, leaving rem sts on a holder.
Work each side of neck separately.
Keeping patt correct, dec 1 st at neck edge of next 4 rows, then on foll 0 [0: 1: 1: 1: 1] alt rows **and at same time** dec 1 st at raglan armhole edge on 2nd and every foll alt row. 8 sts.
Work 1 row, ending with RS facing for next row.

Next row (RS): Using yarn B K4, using yarn A sl 1, K1, psso, K2tog. 6 sts.

Next row: Using yarn A P2, using yarn B P4.
Break off yarn A and cont using yarn B only.

Next row: K3, sl 1, K2tog, psso. 4 sts.

Next row: P4.

Next row: K1, sl 1, K2tog, psso.

Next row: P2.

Next row: K2tog and fasten off.
With RS facing, slip centre 7 [9: 9: 9: 11: 11] sts onto a holder, rejoin yarns to rem sts, using yarn A K to last 6 sts, K2tog, using yarn B K4.
Complete to match first side, reversing shapings.

SLEEVES

Using 4mm (US 6) needles and yarn B cast on 31 [33: 33: 35: 35: 37] sts.
Joining in and breaking off colours as required, cont in fancy rib as folls:

Row 1 (RS): Using yarn B K0 [1: 1: 0: 0: 1], *K1, ytf, sl 1, ytb, K2, rep from * to last 3 [0: 0: 3: 3: 0] sts, (K1, ytf, sl 1, ytb, K1) 1 [0: 0: 1: 1: 0] times.

Row 2: Using yarn B (ytf, sl 1, ytb) 0 [1: 1: 0: 0: 1] times, *K3, ytf, sl 1, ytb, rep from * to last 3 [0: 0: 3: 3: 0] sts, K3 [0: 0: 3: 3: 0].

Rows 3 and 4: Using yarn A, as rows 1 and 2.

Rows 5 and 6: Using yarn C, as rows 1 and 2.

Rows 7 and 8: As rows 3 and 4.

3rd, 4th, 5th and 6th sizes

Rows 9 and 10: Using yarn D, as rows 1 and 2.

Rows 11 and 12: As rows 3 and 4.

All sizes

Change to 4½ mm (US 7) needles.
Beg with a K row, work in st st, shaping sides by inc 1 st at each end of next and every foll 6th row to 41 [43: 49: 39: 41: 51] sts, then on every foll 8th [8th: –: 8th: 8th: 8th] row until there are 43 [47: –: 49: 51: 57] sts.
Cont straight until sleeve meas 17 [20: 23:

25: 27: 30] cm, ending with RS facing for next row.

Shape raglan

Place markers at both ends of last row to denote base of armholes.
Join in yarn B and cont as folls:

6th size only

Next row (RS): Using yarn B K4, using yarn A sl 1, K1, psso, K to last 6 sts, K2tog, using yarn B K4.

Next row: Using yarn B P4, using yarn A P2tog, P to last 6 sts, P2tog tbl, using yarn B P4. 53 sts.

All sizes

Next row (RS): Using yarn B K4, using yarn A sl 1, K1, psso, K to last 6 sts, K2tog, using yarn B K4.

Next row: Using yarn B P4, using yarn A P to last 6 sts, using yarn B P4.
Rep last 2 rows until 11 sts rem.
Work 1 row, ending with RS facing for next row.
Keeping patt and decreases correct as set, cont as folls:

Left sleeve only

Next row (RS): Using yarn B K4, using yarn A sl 1, K1, psso, using yarn B K4. 9 sts.
Cast off 2 sts at beg of next row. 7 sts.

Next row (RS): Using yarn B K4, sl 1, K1, psso, K1. 6 sts.
Cast off 3 sts at beg of next row.

Right sleeve only

Next row (RS): Cast off 3 sts, patt until there are 2 sts on right needle, K2tog, using yarn B K4. 7 sts.
Work 1 row.
Cast off 4 sts at beg of next row.
Work 1 row.

Both sleeves

Cast off rem 3 sts.

MAKING UP

Press as described on the information page.

1st and 2nd sizes

Join raglan seams using back stitch, or mattress stitch if preferred.

Neckband

With RS facing, using 4mm (US 6) needles and yarn A, beg and ending at back opening edge, K10 [11: –: –: –: –] sts from left back holder, pick up and knit 8 sts from left sleeve, 12 sts down left side of neck, K7 [9: –: –: –: –] sts from front, pick up and knit 12 sts up right side of neck, and 8 sts from right sleeve, then

K10 [11: –: –: –: –] sts from right back holder. 67 [71: –: –: –: –] sts.

3rd, 4th, 5th and 6th sizes

Join both front and right back raglan seams using back stitch, or mattress stitch if preferred.

Neckband

With RS facing, using 4mm (US 6) needles and yarn A, pick up and knit 8 sts from left sleeve, 15 sts down left side of neck, K– [–: 9: 9: 11: 11] sts from front, pick up and knit 15 sts up right side of neck, and 8 sts from right sleeve, then K– [–: 25: 25: 27: 27] sts from back dec 1 st at centre. – [–: 79: 79: 83: 83] sts.

All sizes

Row 1 (WS): Using yarn A K1, *ytf, sl 1, ytb, K3, rep from * to last 2 sts, ytf, sl 1, ytb, K1.
Join in yarn C.

Row 2: Using yarn C K3, *ytf, sl 1, ytb, K3, rep from * to end.

Row 3: Using yarn C, as row 1.
Break off yarn C.

Row 4: Using yarn A, as row 2.

Row 5: As row 1.
Join in yarn B.

Row 6: Using yarn B, as row 2.
Using yarn B, cast off in patt.

1st and 2nd sizes

Make button loop and attach button to fasten back neck.

3rd, 4th, 5th and 6th sizes

Join left back raglan and neckband seam.

All sizes

See information page for finishing instructions.

Cardigan

BACK

Work as given for back of sweater to **.
Working all raglan armhole decreases as set by last row, dec 1 st at each end of 4th and every foll 4th row to 43 [49: 53: 57: 61: 61] sts, then on every foll alt row until 21 [23: 25: 25: 27: 27] sts rem.
Work 1 row, end with RS facing for next row.
Break yarn and leave rem sts on a holder.

LEFT FRONT

Using 4mm (US 6) needles and yarn B cast on 25 [28: 30: 31: 33: 34] sts.
Joining in and breaking off colours as required, cont in fancy rib as folls:

Row 1 (RS): Using yarn B K5 [4: 4: 5: 5: 4],

(ytf, sl 1, ytb, K1) 0 [0: 1: 1: 0: 1] times, *K2, ytf, sl 1, ytb, K1, rep from * to end.

Row 2: Using yarn B K3, *ytf, sl 1, ytb, K3, rep from * to last 6 [5: 7: 4: 6: 7] sts, (ytf, sl 1, ytb) 1 [1: 0: 1: 0: 1] times, K1 [0: 2: 0: 1: 2], P4.

Row 3: Using yarn A K0 [0: 0: 1: 1: 0: 0], (ytf, sl 1, ytb) 0 [0: 1: 1: 0: 1] times, K1 [0: 1: 1: 1: 1], *K2, ytf, sl 1, ytb, K1, rep from * to end.

Row 4: Using yarn A K3, *ytf, sl 1, ytb, K3, rep from * to last 6 [5: 7: 4: 6: 7] sts, (ytf, sl 1, ytb) 1 [1: 0: 1: 0: 1] times, K1 [0: 2: 0: 1: 2], using yarn B P4.

Row 5: Using yarn B K4, using yarn C K0 [0: 0: 1: 0: 0], (ytf, sl 1, ytb) 0 [0: 1: 1: 0: 1] times, K1 [0: 1: 1: 1: 1], *K2, ytf, sl 1, ytb, K1, rep from * to end.

Row 6: Using yarn C K3, *ytf, sl 1, ytb, K3, rep from * to last 6 [5: 7: 4: 6: 7] sts, (ytf, sl 1, ytb) 1 [1: 0: 1: 0: 1] times, K1 [0: 2: 0: 1: 2], using yarn B P4.

Rows 7 and 8: As rows 3 and 4.

Row 9: Using yarn B K4, using yarn D K0 [0: 0: 1: 0: 0], (ytf, sl 1, ytb) 0 [0: 1: 1: 0: 1] times, K1 [0: 1: 1: 1: 1], *K2, ytf, sl 1, ytb, K1, rep from * to end.

Row 10: Using yarn D K3, *ytf, sl 1, ytb, K3, rep from * to last 6 [5: 7: 4: 6: 7] sts, (ytf, sl 1, ytb) 1 [1: 0: 1: 0: 1] times, K1 [0: 2: 0: 1: 2], using yarn B P4.

Rows 11 and 12: As rows 3 and 4.

3rd, 4th, 5th and 6th sizes

Rows 13 to 16: As rows 1 to 4.

All sizes

Change to 4½mm (US 7) needles.
Break off yarn C and D and cont as folls:

Row 1 (RS): Using yarn B K4, using yarn A K to end.

Row 2: Using yarn A P to last 4 sts, using yarn B P4.
These 2 rows form patt.
Cont in patt until left front matches back to beg of raglan armhole shaping, ending with RS facing for next row.

Shape raglan armhole

Place marker at end of last row to denote base of armhole.

Next row (RS): Using yarn B K4, using yarn A sl 1, K1, psso, K to end.
Working all raglan armhole decreases as set by last row, dec 1 st at beg of 4th and every foll 4th row to 21 [24: 26: 28: 30: 30] sts, then on every foll alt row until 18 [19: 21: 21: 22: 22] sts rem, ending with **WS** facing for next row.

Shape neck

Keeping patt correct, cast off 3 [4: 4: 4: 5: 5] sts at beg of next row.
15 [15: 17: 17: 17: 17] sts.
Dec 1 st at neck edge of next 3 rows, then on foll 1 [1: 2: 2: 2: 2] alt rows **and at same time** dec 1 st at raglan armhole edge on next and every foll alt row. 8 sts.
Work 1 row, ending with RS facing for next row.
Next row (RS): Using yarn B K4, using yarn A sl 1, K1, psso, K2tog. 6 sts.
Next row: Using yarn A P2, using yarn B P4.
Break off yarn A and cont using yarn B only.
Next row: K3, sl 1, K2tog, psso. 4 sts.
Next row: P4.
Next row: K1, sl 1, K2tog, psso.
Next row: P2.
Next row: K2tog and fasten off.

RIGHT FRONT

Using 4mm (US 6) needles and yarn B cast on 25 [28: 30: 31: 33: 34] sts.
Joining in and breaking off colours as required, cont in fancy rib as folls:
Row 1 (RS): Using yarn B K1, ytf, sl 1, ytb, K1, *K2, ytf, sl 1, ytb, K1, rep from * to last 6 [5: 7: 4: 6: 7] sts, K6 [5: 2: 4: 6: 2], (ytf, sl 1, ytb, K4) 0 [0: 1: 0: 0: 1] times.
Row 2: Using yarn B P4, K1 [0: 2: 3: 1: 2], *ytf, sl 1, ytb, K3, rep from * to end.
Row 3: Using yarn A K1, ytf, sl 1, ytb, K1, *K2, ytf, sl 1, ytb, K1, rep from * to last 6 [5: 7: 4: 6: 7] sts, K2 [1: 2: 0: 2: 2], (ytf, sl 1, ytb) 0 [0: 1: 0: 0: 1] times, using yarn B K4.

Row 4: Using yarn B P4, using yarn A K1 [0: 2: 3: 1: 2], *ytf, sl 1, ytb, K3, rep from * to end.
Row 5: Using yarn C K1, ytf, sl 1, ytb, K1, *K2, ytf, sl 1, ytb, K1, rep from * to last 6 [5: 7: 4: 6: 7] sts, K2 [1: 2: 0: 2: 2], (ytf, sl 1, ytb, K4) 0 [0: 1: 0: 0: 1] times, using yarn B K4.
Row 6: Using yarn B P4, using yarn C K1 [0: 2: 3: 1: 2], *ytf, sl 1, ytb, K3, rep from * to end.
Rows 7 and 8: As rows 3 and 4.
Row 9: Using yarn D K1, ytf, sl 1, ytb, K1, *K2, ytf, sl 1, ytb, K1, rep from * to last 6 [5: 7: 4: 6: 7] sts, K2 [1: 2: 0: 2: 2], (ytf, sl 1, ytb, K4) 0 [0: 1: 0: 0: 1] times, using yarn B K4.
Row 10: Using yarn B P4, using yarn D K1 [0: 2: 3: 1: 2], *ytf, sl 1, ytb, K3, rep from * to end.
Rows 11 and 12: As rows 3 and 4.
3rd, 4th, 5th and 6th sizes
Rows 13 to 16: As rows 1 to 4.
All sizes
Change to 4½mm (US 7) needles.
Break off yarn C and D and cont as folls:
Row 1 (RS): Using yarn A K to last 4 sts, using yarn B K4.
Row 2: Using yarn B P4, using yarn A P to end.
These 2 rows form patt.
Complete to match left front, reversing shapings.

SLEEVES

Work as given for sleeves of sweater.

MAKING UP

Press as described on the information page.
Join raglan seams using back stitch, or mattress stitch if preferred.

Neckband

With RS facing, using 4mm (US 6) needles and yarn A, beg and ending at front opening edge, pick up and knit 15 [16: 17: 17: 18: 18] sts up right side of neck, 8 sts from right sleeve, 21 [23: 25: 25: 27: 27] sts from back, 8 sts from left sleeve, then 15 [16: 17: 17: 18: 18] sts down left side of neck.
67 [71: 75: 75: 79: 79] sts.
**Row 1 (WS): Using yarn A K1, *ytf, sl 1, ytb, K3, rep from * to last 2 sts, ytf, sl 1, ytb, K1.
Join in yarn C.
Row 2: Using yarn C K3, *ytf, sl 1, ytb, K3, rep from * to end.
Row 3: Using yarn C, as row 1.
Break off yarn C.
Row 4: Using yarn A, as row 2.
Row 5: As row 1.
Break off yarn A and join in yarn B.

Row 6: Using yarn B, as row 2.
Using yarn B, cast off in patt.**
Button band
With RS facing, using 4mm (US 6) needles and yarn A, pick up and knit 51 [59: 67: 67: 71: 75] sts evenly along one front opening edge (left front for a girl, or right front for a boy), between top of neckband and cast-on edge.
Work as given for neckband from ** to **.
Buttonhole band
Work as given for button band, picking up sts along other front opening edge and with the addition of 5 buttonholes worked in row 2 as folls:
Row 2 (buttonhole row) (RS): Patt 3 sts, *yrn, work 2 tog (to make a buttonhole), patt 9 [11: 13: 13: 14: 15] sts, rep from * to last 4 sts, yrn, work 2 tog (to make 5th buttonhole), patt 2 sts.

See information page for finishing instructions.

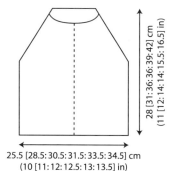

25.5 [28.5: 30.5: 31.5: 33.5: 34.5] cm
(10 [11: 12: 12.5: 13: 13.5] in)

28 [31: 36: 36: 39: 42] cm
(11 [12: 14: 14: 15.5: 16.5] in)

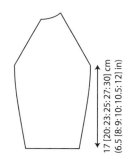

17 [20: 23: 25: 27: 30] cm
(6.5 [8: 9: 10: 10.5: 12] in)

ODETTE BLANKET

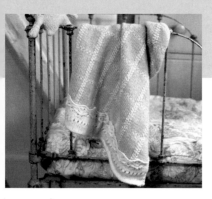

YARN
Rowan Soft Baby
A Angel   002   2 x 50gm
B Cloud   001   1 x 50gm

NEEDLES
1 pair 4½mm (no 7) (US 7) needles
4mm (no 8) (US 6) circular needle

FINISHED SIZE
Completed blanket measures 46 cm (18 in) wide and 63 cm (25 in) long.

TENSION
20 sts and 28 rows to 10 cm measured over stocking stitch using 4½mm (US 7) needles.

SPECIAL ABBREVIATIONS
sl 2 = slip 2 sts; **p2sso** = pass 2 slipped sts over.

BLANKET (worked from top downwards)
Using 4½mm (US 7) needles and yarn B cast on 119 sts.
Work in g st for 2 rows, ending with RS facing for next row.
Work border patt as folls:
Row 1 (RS): K3, *sl 1, K1, psso, sl 2, K3tog, p2sso, K2tog, K4, rep from * to last 12 sts, sl 1, K1, psso, sl 2, K3tog, p2sso, K2tog, K3. 65 sts.
Row 2: K1, P3, *yrn, P1, yrn, P6, rep from * to last 5 sts, yrn, P1, yrn, P3, K1. 83 sts.
Row 3: K1, yfwd, *K2, sl 1, K1, psso, K1, K2tog, K2, yfwd, rep from * to last st, K1. 75 sts.
Row 4: K1, P1, *yrn, P2, yrn, P3, yrn, P2, yrn, P1, rep from * to last st, K1. 111 sts.
Row 5: K2, yfwd, K1, *yfwd, sl 1, K1, psso, K1, sl 1, K2tog, psso, K1, K2tog, (yfwd, K1) 3 times, rep from * to last 12 sts, yfwd, sl 1, K1, psso, K1, sl 1, K2tog, psso, K1, K2tog, yfwd,

K1, yfwd, K2.
Row 6: K1, P to last st, K1.
Row 7: K5, *yfwd, sl 2, K3tog, p2sso, yfwd, K7, rep from * to last 10 sts, yfwd, sl 2, K3tog, p2sso, yfwd, K5. 93 sts.
Row 8: As row 6.
Row 9: Knit.
Rows 10 and 11: As rows 8 and 9.
Row 12: As row 6.
Row 13 (eyelet row): K1, *yfwd, K2tog, rep from * to end.
Row 14: K1, P to last st, K1.
Row 15: Knit.
Rep last 2 rows until blanket meas 10 cm, ending with RS facing for next row.
Next row (fold line row) (RS of border, WS of main section): K1, P13, (P2tog, P29) twice, P2tog, P to last st, K1. 90 sts.
Break off yarn B and join in yarn A.
Change to 4½ mm (US 7) needles.
Beg and ending rows as indicated, using the **fairisle** technique as described on the information page and repeating the 20 row patt repeat throughout, cont in patt from

chart, which is worked entirely in st st beg with a K row, until blanket meas 56 cm **from fold line row**, ending with RS of main section facing for next row.
Keeping patt correct, dec 1 st at each end of next and foll 4 alt rows, then on foll 7 rows, ending with RS facing for next row.
Cast off rem 66 sts.

MAKING UP
Press as described on the information page.
Following chart, swiss darn vertical lines onto main section.
Edging
Using 4mm (US 6) circular needle and yarn B, beg and ending at fold line row, pick up and knit 128 sts down first row-end edge of main section to cast-off edge, 66 sts from cast-off edge, then 128 sts up other row-end edge of main section to fold line row. 322 sts.
Work in g st for 2 rows.
Cast off knitwise (on WS).
Fold border over onto RS of main section along fold line row and secure at side edges.

Key   □ A   □ B   ⊡ Swiss darn using B

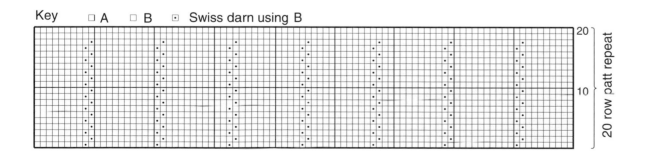

20 row patt repeat

Key

□ A - K on RS, P on WS

□ B - K on RS, P on WS

⊡ swiss darn using B

HANNAH

●

YARN

	3-6	6-12				months
			1-2	2-3	3-4	4-5	years
To fit chest						
	46	51	56	58	61	64	cm
	18	20	22	23	24	25	in

Rowan Soft Baby and Kidsilk Haze

A BabyCosy 004						
	2	2	3	3	3	3	x 50gm
B BabyPrincess 003						
	1	1	1	1	1	1	x 50gm
C KSHMajestic 589						
	1	1	1	1	1	1	x 25gm
D KSHDewberry 600						
	1	1	1	1	1	1	x 25gm
E KSHGrace 580						
	1	1	1	1	1	1	x 25gm

NEEDLES

1 pair 4mm (no 8) (US 6) needles
1 pair 4½mm (no 7) (US 7) needles
2.50 [2.50: 3.00: 3.00: 3.50: 3.50]mm
(no 12 [12: 11: 11: 9: 9]) (US C2 [C2: D3: D3: E4: E4]) crochet hook

BUTTONS – 1st and 2nd sizes: 1

TENSION

20 sts and 28 rows to 10 cm measured over stocking stitch using 4½mm (US 7) needles and yarn A.

CROCHET ABBREVIATIONS

ss = slip stitch; **ch** = chain; **dc** = double crochet; **htr** = half treble; **tr** = treble; **dtr** = double treble; **sp(s)** = space(s).

BACK

Using 4½mm (US 7) needles and yarn A cast on 57 [63: 67: 69: 73: 75] sts.
Beg with a K row, work in st st, shaping sides by dec 1 st at each end of 11th and every foll 10th [12th: 14th: 16th: 18th: 20th] row until 51 [57: 61: 63: 67: 69] sts rem.
Cont straight until back meas 14 [16: 19: 20: 22: 23] cm, ending with RS facing for next row.
Shape armholes
Cast off 3 sts at beg of next 2 rows.
45 [51: 55: 57: 61: 63] sts.
Dec 1 st at each end of next 3 [5: 5: 5: 5: 5] rows, then on foll 2 alt rows.
35 [37: 41: 43: 47: 49] sts.★★
1st and 2nd sizes
Work 1 row, ending with RS facing for next row.
Divide for back opening
Next row (RS): K17 [18: -: -: -: -] and turn, leaving rem sts on a holder.
Work each side of neck separately.
Next row (WS): K1, P to end.
This row sets the sts – back opening edge st now in g st with all other sts still in st st.
Cont as set until armhole meas 11 [12: -: -: -: -] cm, ending with RS facing for next row.
Shape shoulder
Cast off 3 sts at beg of next row, then 4 sts at beg of foll row.
Break yarn and leave rem 10 [11: -: -: -: -] sts on a holder.
With RS facing, rejoin yarn to rem sts, K2tog, K to end.
17 [18: -: -: -: -] sts.
Next row (WS): P to last st, K1.
Complete to match first side, reversing shapings.
3rd, 4th, 5th and 6th sizes
Cont straight until armhole meas – [-: 13: 14: 14: 15] cm, ending with RS facing for next row.

Shape shoulders

Cast off – [-: 4: 4: 5: 5] sts at beg of next 2 rows, then – [-: 4: 4: 5: 5: 6] sts at beg of foll 2 rows.
Break yarn and leave rem – [-: 25: 25: 27: 27] sts on a holder.

FRONT

Work as given for back to ★★.
Cont straight until 16 [16: 18: 18: 18: 18] rows less have been worked than on back to beg of shoulder shaping, ending with RS facing for next row.
Shape neck
Next row (RS): K14 [14: 16: 17: 18: 19] and turn, leaving rem sts on a holder.
Work each side of neck separately.
Dec 1 st at neck edge of next 4 rows, then on foll 2 [2: 3: 3: 3: 3] alt rows, then on foll 4th row.
7 [7: 8: 9: 10: 11] sts.
Work 3 rows, ending with RS facing for next row.
Shape shoulder
Cast off 3 [3: 4: 4: 5: 5] sts at beg of next row.
Work 1 row.
Cast off rem 4 [4: 4: 5: 5: 6] sts.
With RS facing, slip centre 7 [9: 9: 9: 11: 11] sts onto a holder, rejoin yarn to rem sts, K to end.
Complete to match first side, reversing shapings.

SLEEVES

Using 4½mm (US 7) needles and yarn A cast on 32 [34: 34: 36: 36: 38] sts.
Beg with a K row, work in st st, shaping sides by inc 1 st at each end of 13th [11th: 9th: 9th: 9th: 9th] and every foll 16th [14th: 10th: 10th: 10th: 10th] row to 36 [40: 38: 46: 40: 46] sts, then on every foll – [-: 12th: –: 12th: 12th] row until there are – [-: 42: –: 46: 50] sts.
Cont straight until sleeve meas 14 [17: 20: 22: 24: 27] cm, ending with RS facing for next row.
Shape top
Cast off 3 sts at beg of next 2 rows.
30 [34: 36: 40: 40: 44] sts.
Dec 1 st at each end of next 3 rows, then on

foll 6 [6: 7: 7: 7: 7] alt rows, then on foll 1 [3: 3: 5: 5: 7] rows, ending with RS facing for next row.
Cast off rem 10 sts.

MAKING UP

Press as described on the information page.
1st and 2nd sizes
Join both shoulder seams using back stitch, or mattress stitch if preferred.
Neckband
With RS facing, using 4mm (US 6) needles and yarn B, beg and ending at back opening edge, K10 [11: -: -: -: -] sts from left back holder, pick up and knit 16 sts down left side of neck, K7 [9: -: -: -: -] sts from front, pick up and knit 16 sts up right side of neck, then K10 [11: -: -: -: -] sts from right back holder.
59 [63: -: -: -: -] sts.
Row 1 (WS): K to last 3 sts, yfwd (to make a buttonhole), K2tog, K1.
Rows 2 and 3: Knit.
Work picot cast-off as folls: cast off 2 sts, *slip st on right needle back onto left needle, cast on 2 sts, cast off 4 sts, rep from * until all sts are cast off.
Attach button to correspond with buttonhole.
3rd, 4th, 5th and 6th sizes
Join right shoulder seam using back stitch, or mattress stitch if preferred.
Neckband
With RS facing, using 4mm (US 6) needles and yarn B, pick up and knit 18 sts down left side of neck, K– [-: 9: 9: 11: 11] sts from front, pick up and knit 18 sts up right side of neck, then K– [-: 25: 25: 27: 27] sts from back.
– [-: 70: 70: 74: 74] sts.
Work in g st for 3 rows, dec 1 st at end of last row and ending with RS facing for next row.
– [-: 69: 69: 73: 73] sts.
Work picot cast-off as folls: cast off 2 sts, *slip st on right needle back onto left needle, cast on 2 sts, cast off 4 sts, rep from * until all sts are cast off.
All sizes
See information page for finishing instructions, setting in sleeves using the set-in method.

Edging

Using 4mm (US 6) needles and yarn B cast on 5 sts.

Row 1 (RS): K3, (yfwd) twice, K2.

Row 2: K2, K into front and back of double yfwd of previous row, K3.
7 sts.

Row 3: K7.

Row 4: Cast off 2 sts, K to end. 5 sts.

These 4 rows form patt.

Cont in patt until edging fits around entire lower edge of body, ending after patt row 4. Cast off.

Join ends of edging, then slip stitch straight edge in place to cast-on edges of back and front.

In same way, make and attach edging to lower edges of sleeves.

Large flower

With crochet hook and yarn C DOUBLE, make 7 ch and join with a ss to form a ring.

Round 1 (RS): 1 ch (does NOT count as st), 14 dc into ring, ss to first dc.

Break off yarn C and join in yarn D DOUBLE.

Round 2: 6 ch (counts as first tr and 3 ch), miss first 2 dc, ★1 tr into next dc, 3 ch, miss 1 dc, rep from ★ to end, ss to 3rd of 6 ch at beg of round. 7 ch sps.

Round 3: 1 ch (does NOT count as st), (1 dc, 1 htr, 1 tr, 3 dtr, 1 tr, 1 htr and 1 dc) into each ch sp to end, ss to first dc.
7 petals.

Fasten off.

Medium flower

With crochet hook and yarn C DOUBLE, make 6 ch and join with a ss to form a ring.

Round 1 (RS): 1 ch (does NOT count as st), 12 dc into ring, ss to first dc.

Break off yarn C and join in yarn E DOUBLE.

Round 2: 6 ch (counts as first tr and 3 ch), miss first 2 dc, ★1 tr into next dc, 3 ch, miss 1 dc, rep from ★ to end, ss to 3rd of 6 ch at beg of round. 6 ch sps.

Round 3: 1 ch (does NOT count as st), (1 dc, 1 htr, 1 tr, 3 dtr, 1 tr, 1 htr and 1 dc) into each ch sp to end, ss to first dc. 6 petals.

Fasten off.

Small flower

With crochet hook and yarn C DOUBLE, make 5 ch and join with a ss to form a ring.

Round 1 (RS): 1 ch (does NOT count as st), 10 dc into ring, ss to first dc.

Break off yarn C and join in yarn D DOUBLE.

Round 2: 5 ch (counts as first htr and 3 ch), miss first 2 dc, ★1 htr into next dc, 3 ch, miss 1 dc, rep from ★ to end, ss to 2nd of 5 ch at beg of round. 5 ch sps.

Round 3: 1 ch (does NOT count as st), (1 dc, 1 htr, 1 tr, 3 dtr, 1 tr, 1 htr and 1 dc) into each ch sp to end, ss to first dc.
5 petals.

Fasten off.

Using photograph as a guide, sew flowers onto front. Using yarn C DOUBLE and chain st, embroider stems and leaves as in photograph.

28 [31:35:37:39:41] cm
(11 [12:14:14.5:15.5:16] in)

25.5 [28.5:30.5:31.5:33.5:34.5] cm
(10 [11:12:12.5:13:13.5] in)

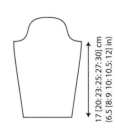

17 [20:23:25:27:30] cm
(6.5 [8:9:10:10.5:12] in)

JASPER

YARN

3-6	6-12					months
		1-2	2-3	3-4	4-5	years

To fit chest

46	51	56	58	61	64	cm
18	20	22	23	24	25	in

Rowan Soft Baby and 4 ply Soft

A Baby Cloud 001

2	3	3	3	4	4	x 50gm

B Baby Angel 002

1	1	1	1	1	1	x 50gm

C *4 ply Rainc.387

1	1	1	1	1	1	x 50gm

Use 4 ply Soft DOUBLE throughout

NEEDLES

1 pair 4mm (no 8) (US 6) needles
1 pair 4½mm (no 7) (US 7) needles

BUTTONS – 1st and 2nd sizes: 1

EXTRAS – 3 buttons for eyes (00392,00393 and 00395) and oddment of Soft Baby (Princess 003) for tongue embroidery

TENSION

20 sts and 28 rows to 10 cm measured over stocking stitch using 4½mm (US 7) needles and yarn A.

BACK

Using 4½mm (US 7) needles and yarn A cast on 51 [57: 61: 63: 67: 69] sts.
Beg with a K row, work in st st until back meas 15 [17: 21: 21: 23: 25] cm, ending with RS facing for next row.
Shape raglan armholes
Cast off 3 sts at beg of next 2 rows.
45 [51: 55: 57: 61: 63] sts.
Next row (RS): K1, sl 1, K1, psso, K to last 3 sts, K2tog, K1.
Work 3 rows.
Rep last 4 rows 2 [2: 4: 4: 3: 2] times more.
39 [45: 45: 47: 53: 57] sts.
2nd size
Next row (RS): K1, sl 1, K1, psso, K to last 3 sts, K2tog, K1.
43 sts.
Work 1 row.
1st and 2nd sizes
Divide for back opening
Next row (RS): (K1, sl 1, K1, psso)1 [0: –: –: –: –] times, K16 [21: –: –: –: –] and turn, leaving rem sts on a holder.
18 [21: –: –: –: –] sts.
Work each side of neck separately.
Next row (WS): K1, P to end.
This row sets the sts – back opening edge st now in g st with all other sts still in st st.
Working all raglan armhole decreases as set, dec 1 st at raglan armhole edge of 3rd [next: –: –: –: –] and foll 4th [alt: –: –: –: –] row, then on every foll alt row until 10 [11: –: –: –: –] sts rem.
Work 1 row, ending with RS facing for next row.
Break yarn and leave rem 10 [11: –: –: –: –] sts on a holder.
With RS facing, rejoin yarn to rem sts, K2tog, K to last 3 [0: –: –: –: –] sts, (K2tog, K1) 1 [0: –: –: –: –] times.
18 [21: –: –: –: –] sts.
Next row (WS): P to last st, K1.
Complete to match first side, reversing shapings.
3rd, 4th, 5th and 6th sizes
Working all raglan armhole decreases as set, dec 1 st at each end of next and every foll alt row until – [–: 25: 25: 27: 27] sts rem.
Work 1 row, ending with RS facing for next row.
Break yarn and leave rem – [–: 25: 25: 27: 27] sts on a holder.

FRONT

Using 4½mm (US 7) needles and yarn A cast on 51 [57: 61: 63: 67: 69] sts.
Beg with a K row, work in st st for 18 [24: 34: 34: 40: 46] rows, ending with RS facing for next row.
Place chart
Using the **intarsia** technique as described on the information page, place chart as folls:
Next row (RS): K11 [14: 16: 17: 19: 20], work next 30 sts as row 1 of chart, K to end.
Next row: P10 [13: 15: 16: 18: 19], work next 30 sts as row 2 of chart, P to end.
These 2 rows set position of chart.
Working in patt as set until all 26 rows of chart have been completed and then completing front using yarn A **only**, cont as folls:
Cont straight until front matches back to beg of raglan armhole shaping, ending with RS facing for next row.
Shape raglan armholes
Cast off 3 sts at beg of next 2 rows.
45 [51: 55: 57: 61: 63] sts.
Working all raglan armhole decreases as set by back, dec 1 st at each end of next and every foll 4th row to 35 [41: 43: 45: 51: 55] sts, then on foll 0 [1: 0: 1: 3: 5] alt rows.
35 [39: 43: 43: 45: 45] sts.
Work 1 row, ending with RS facing for next row.
Shape neck
Next row (RS): (K1, sl 1, K1, psso) 0 [1: 1: 1: 1: 1] times, K14 [12: 14: 14: 14: 14] and turn, leaving rem sts on a holder.
Work each side of neck separately.
Dec 1 st at neck edge of next 4 rows, then on foll 2 [2: 3: 3: 3: 3] alt rows **and at same time** dec 1 st at raglan armhole edge on 2nd and every foll alt row.
4 sts.
Work 1 row, ending with RS facing for next row.
Next row (RS): K1, sl 1, K2tog, psso.
Next row: P2.
Next row: K2tog and fasten off.
With RS facing, slip centre 7 [9: 9: 9: 11: 11] sts onto a holder, rejoin yarn to rem sts, K to last 0 [3: 3: 3: 3: 3] sts, (K2tog, K1) 0 [1: 1: 1: 1: 1] times.
Complete to match first side, reversing shapings.

SLEEVES

Using 4½mm (US 7) needles and yarn A cast on 32 [34: 34: 36: 36: 38] sts.
Beg with a K row, work in st st, shaping sides by inc 1 st at each end of 7th [7th: 5th: 5th: 7th: 9th] and every foll 8th [10th: 6th: 6th: 8th: 10th] row to 42 [44: 44: 42: 52: 50] sts, then on every foll – [–: 8th: 8th: –: 12th] row until there are – [–: 50: 52: –: 52] sts.
Cont straight until sleeve meas 17 [20: 23: 25: 27: 30] cm, ending with RS facing for next row.
Shape raglan
Cast off 3 sts at beg of next 2 rows.
36 [38: 44: 46: 46: 46] sts.
Working all raglan decreases as set by back, dec 1 st at each end of next and every foll 4th row to 30 [32: 40: 42: 42: 42] sts, then on every foll alt row until 10 sts rem.
Work 1 row, ending with RS facing for next row.
Left sleeve only
Dec 1 st at each end of next row.
8 sts.
Cast off 3 sts at beg of next row.
5 sts.
Next row (RS): K1, sl 1, K1, psso, K2tog.
3 sts.
Next row: P2tog, P1.
Right sleeve only
Cast off 3 sts at beg and dec 1 st at end of next row. 6 sts.
Dec 1 st at end of next row.
5 sts.
Next row (RS): (K2tog) twice, K1.
3 sts.
Next row: P1, P2tog.
Both sleeves
Next row (RS): K2tog and fasten off.

MAKING UP

Press as described on the information page.
Sleeve trim (make 2)
Using 4½mm (US 7) needles and yarn C DOUBLE cast on 5 sts.
Row 1 (RS): Knit.
Row 2: K1, P3, K1.
Rep these 2 rows until trim fits up centre of

sleeve to neck shaping, ending with RS facing for next row.

Left sleeve trim only
Dec 1 st at end of next row and at same edge on foll 3 rows.

Right sleeve trim only
Dec 1 st at beg of next row and at same edge on foll 3 rows.

Both sleeve trims
Fasten off rem st.
With WS of trim against RS of sleeve, lay sleeve trim centrally along sleeve, matching shaped edges at top, and sew in place.

1st and 2nd sizes
Leaving seams open at underarm, join raglan seams using back stitch, or mattress stitch if preferred.

Collar
With RS facing, using 4mm (US 6) needles and yarn A, beg and ending at back opening edge, K10 [11: –: –: –: –] sts from left back holder, pick up and knit 6 sts from left sleeve (working through trim and sleeve), 12 sts down left side of neck, K7 [9: –: –: –: –] sts from front, pick up and knit 12 sts up right side of neck, and 6 sts from right sleeve, then K10 [11: –: –: –: –] sts from right back holder.
63 [67: –: –: –: –] sts.

Row 1 (WS): K1, *P1, K1, rep from * to end.
Row 2: K2, *P1, K1, rep from * to last st, K1.
Rep last 2 rows once more.
Next row (WS): K1, P to last st, K1.
Next row: Knit.
Rep last 2 rows once more.
Cast off in patt.
Make button loop and attach button to fasten back neck.

3rd, 4th, 5th and 6th sizes
Leaving seams open at underarm, join both front and right back raglan seams using back stitch, or mattress stitch if preferred.

Collar
With RS facing, using 4mm (US 6) needles and yarn A, pick up and knit 6 sts from left sleeve, 14 sts down left side of neck, K– [–: 9: 9: 11: 11] sts from front, pick up and knit 14 sts up right side of neck, and 6 sts from right sleeve, then K– [–: 25: 25: 27: 27] sts from back dec 1 st at centre.
– [–: 73: 73: 77: 77] sts.

Row 1 (WS): P1, *K1, P1, rep from * to end.
Row 2: K1, *P1, K1, rep from * to end.
Rep last 2 rows twice more, ending with **WS** facing for next row.
Beg with a P row, work in st st for 4 rows.
Cast off purlwise.

Leaving seam open at underarm, join left back raglan seam, reversing seam for st st roll.

All sizes
Join side seams.

Side trim (make 2)
Work as given for sleeve trim, working a strip long enough to fit from cast-on edge of back and front to underarm.

With WS of trim against RS of body, lay side trim over side seam and sew in place.
See information page for finishing instructions.

Decoration
Using oddments of contrast yarns and photograph as a guide, embroider mouth onto motif in stem st, then tongue in fly stitch.
Securely attach button eyes as in photograph.

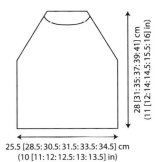

28 [31: 35: 37: 39: 41] cm
(11 [12: 14: 14.5: 15.5: 16] in)

25.5 [28.5: 30.5: 31.5: 33.5: 34.5] cm
(10 [11: 12: 12.5: 13: 13.5] in)

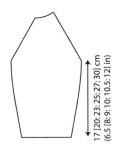

17 [20: 23: 25: 27: 30] cm
(6.5 [8: 9: 10: 10.5: 12] in)

Key ☐ A ☐ B

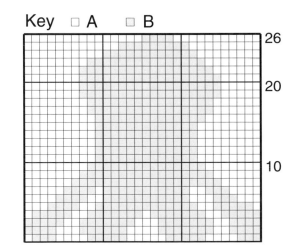

26

20

10

AGNES TOY

●

YARN
Rowan Soft Baby
1 x 50gm
(photographed in Princess 003)
Oddment of Rowan 4 ply Soft in contrast colour (387) for legs and oddments of Rowan Baby Soft (008) for beak

CROCHET HOOK
4.00mm (no 8) (US G6) crochet hook

EXTRAS – Washable toy filling, 2 x 00333 buttons for eyes.

FINISHED SIZE
Completed toy is approx 13 cm (5 ins) tall, excluding legs.

TENSION
14 sts and 17 rows to 10 cm measured over double crochet fabric using 4.00mm (US G6) hook.

CROCHET ABBREVIATIONS
ch = chain; **ss** = slip stitch; **dc** = double crochet.

FRONT and BACK (both alike)
Using 4.00mm (US G6) crochet hook, make 8 ch.
Round 1 (RS): 1 dc into 2nd ch from hook, 1 dc into next ch, 1 ss into next ch, turn, 1 ch (does NOT count as st), 1 dc into next ss, 1 dc into next dc, 2 dc into next dc, working into other side of foundation ch 2 dc into same ch as first dc of this round, 1 dc into next ch, 1 ss into next ch, turn, 1 ch (does NOT count as st), (1 dc into each of next 2 sts, 2 dc into next dc) twice, 1 dc into each of next 2 sts, continuing along foundation ch 1 dc into each of next 3 ch, 4 dc into last ch, working back along other side of foundation ch, 1 dc into each of next 3 ch, ss to next dc.
Round 2: 1 ch (does NOT count as st), 1 dc into each of first 4 dc, 2 dc into each of next 2 dc, 1 dc into each of next 8 dc, 2 dc into each of next 2 dc, 1 dc into each of last 4 dc, ss to first dc.
24 sts.
Round 3: 1 ch (does NOT count as st), 1 dc into each of first 3 dc, 2 dc into next dc, 1 dc into next dc, 2 dc into each of next 2 dc, 1 dc into next dc, 2 dc into next dc, 1 dc into each of next 7 dc, 2 dc into each of next 4 dc, 1 dc into each of last 4 dc, ss to first dc.
32 sts.
Round 4: 1 ch (does NOT count as st), 1 dc into each dc to end, ss to first dc.
Round 5: 1 ch (does NOT count as st), 1 dc into each of first 2 dc, 2 dc into next dc, 1 dc into next dc, 2 dc into each of next 2 dc, 1 dc into each of next 4 dc, 2 dc into each of next 2 dc, 1 dc into next dc, 2 dc into next dc, 1 dc into each of next 8 dc, 2 dc into each of next 4 dc, 1 dc into each of next 6 dc, ss to first dc.
42 sts.
Round 6: As round 4.
Round 7: 1 ch (does NOT count as st), 1 dc into each of first 2 dc, (2 dc into next dc, 1 dc into next dc) 3 times, 2 dc into next dc, 1 dc into each of next 4 dc, (2 dc into next dc, 1 dc into next dc) 3 times, 2 dc into next dc, 1 dc into each of next 9 dc, 2 dc into each of next 6 dc, 1 dc into each of next 7 dc, ss to first dc. 56 sts.
Round 8: As round 4.
Fasten off.

WINGS (make 2)
Using 4.00mm (US G6) crochet hook, make 5 ch.
Row 1 (RS): 1 dc into 2nd ch from hook, 1 dc into each of next 2 ch, 3 dc into last ch, working back along other side of foundation ch, 1 dc into each of next 3 ch, turn.
9 sts.
Row 2: 1 ch (does NOT count as st), 1 dc into each of first 4 dc, 3 dc into next dc, 1 dc into each of last 4 dc, turn.
11 sts.
Row 3: 1 ch (does NOT count as st), 1 dc into each of first 5 dc, 3 dc into next dc, 1 dc into each of last 5 dc, turn.
13 sts.
Row 4: 1 ch (does NOT count as st), 1 dc into each of first 5 dc, 2 dc into each of next 3 dc, 1 dc into each of last 5 dc.
16 sts.
Fasten off.

MAKING UP
Press as described on the information page. Sew back and front together, leaving an opening to insert toy filling. Insert toy filling and close opening. Sew straight ends of wings to sides of chick.
Using photograph as a guide and yellow yarn, embroider straight stitch beak. Attach buttons to form eyes.
Legs (both alike)
Using 4.00mm (US G6) crochet hook and oddment of 4 ply Soft DOUBLE, make 11 ch, ss into 6th ch from hook, 7 ch, ss into same ch as before, 5 ch, ss into same ch as before, 1 dc into each of next 5 ch and fasten off.
Attach ends of legs to lower edge of chick as in photograph.

JASPER MOBILE
●●

YARN
Rowan Soft Baby

A Cloud   001   1   x 50gm
B Angel   002   1   x 50gm
Oddment of same yarn in contrast colour
(003) for tongue embroidery and oddment of
4 ply Soft (387) for mouth embroidery.

NEEDLES
1 pair 4mm (no 8) (US 6) needles
3.50mm (no 9) (US E4) crochet hook

EXTRAS – Washable toy filling, 12 buttons,
wooden (or metal) ring 46 cm (18 ins) in
diameter, 6 m of 4 cm (1½in) wide ribbon,
3.60 m of narrow ribbon and metal curtain
ring.

FINISHED SIZE
Completed knitted monster is approx 11 cm
(4¼ins) tall.

TENSION
Based on a stocking stitch tension of 20 sts
and 28 rows to 10 cm using 4½mm (US 7)
needles.

Monsters (make 4)

FRONT
Left arm
Using 4mm (US 6) needles cast on 3 sts.
Row 1 (WS): Purl.
Row 2: Inc in first st, K to last st, inc in
last st. 5 sts.
Row 3: Inc in first st, P to end. 6 sts.
Row 4: Knit.
Row 5: Inc in first st, P to end. 7 sts.
Row 6: Cast off 2 sts, K to last st, inc in last st.
Break yarn and leave rem 6 sts on a holder.
Right leg
Using 4mm (US 6) needles cast on 6 sts.
Row 1 (RS): Knit.
Row 2: Inc in first st, P to last st, inc in
last st. 8 sts.
Row 3: Inc in first st, K to end. 9 sts.
Row 4: P2tog, P to end.
Break yarn and leave rem 8 sts on a holder.
Left leg
Using 4mm (US 6) needles cast on 5 sts.
Row 1 (RS): Knit.
Row 2: Inc in first st, P to last st, inc in
last st. 7 sts.
Row 3: K to last st, inc in last st. 8 sts.
Row 4: Inc in first st, P to last 2 sts, P2tog.
Join legs
Row 5 (RS): Work across sts of left leg as
folls: K to last st, inc in last st, now with RS
facing work across sts of right leg as folls:

K to last 2 sts, K2tog. 16 sts.
Row 6: P2tog, P to last 2 sts, P2tog. 14 sts.
Row 7: Knit.
Row 8: P to last 2 sts, P2tog. 13 sts.
Row 9: Knit.
Break yarn and leave rem 13 sts on a holder.
Right arm
Using 4mm (US 6) needles cast on 2 sts.
Row 1 (RS): Knit.
Row 2: Inc once in each st. 4 sts.
Row 3: Inc in first st, K to end. 5 sts.
Row 4: P to last st, inc in last st. 6 sts.
Row 5: Inc in first st, K to last 2 sts, K2tog.
Row 6: Cast off 2 sts, P to last st, inc in
last st. 5 sts.
Row 7: Inc in first st, K to last 2 sts, K2tog.
Rows 8 and 9: As rows 6 and 7. 4 sts.
Join arms to body
Row 10 (WS): Work across sts of right arm
as folls: P2tog, P1, inc in last st, now with WS
facing work across sts of body as folls: P to
last st, inc in last st, now with WS facing work
across sts of left arm as folls: P to last 2 sts,
P2tog. 23 sts.
Row 11: Cast off 2 sts, K to last 2 sts, K2tog.
20 sts.
Row 12: P2tog, P to last 2 sts, P2tog. 18 sts.
Row 13: K2tog, K to last 2 sts, K2tog. 16 sts.
Row 14: Purl.
Row 15: Knit.
Rows 16 and 17: As rows 14 and 15.
Row 18: Inc in first st, P to end. 17 sts.
Row 19: Inc in first st, K to end. 18 sts.
Row 20: As row 18. 19 sts.
Row 21: Knit.
Row 22: As row 18. 20 sts.
Row 23: Knit.

Row 24: Purl.
Rows 25 and 26: As rows 23 and 24.
Row 27: Knit.
Row 28: P2tog, P to last 2 sts, P2tog. 18 sts.
Row 29: Cast off 2 sts, K to last 2 sts, K2tog.
15 sts.
Row 30: Cast off 2 sts, P to last 2 sts, P2tog.
Cast off rem 12 sts.

BACK
Work as given for front, but reading K for P
and P for K to reverse shape of knitted piece.

MAKING UP
Press as described on the information page.
Sew front and back of each monster together
around entire outer edge, leaving an opening
to insert toy filling. Insert toy filling, then
close opening.
Using oddment of Soft Baby and 4 ply Soft
and photograph as a guide, embroider mouth
onto front in stem st, and tongue in satin
stitch. For eyes, attach 3 buttons securely to
each monster as in photograph.
Wrap length of ribbon around wooden ring
so that it is completely covered and secure in
place. From narrow ribbon, cut four 90 cm
lengths for hanging strips. Join centres of
hanging strips and attach curtain ring at this
point. Attach ends of these ribbons to
wooden ring at four evenly spaced points
around ring. Using 3.00 mm (US E4) crochet
hook and same colour yarn as each monster,
make 4 lengths of chain, each 18 cm long,
and attach one to each monster. Attach other
end to wooden ring, ensuring mobile is
balanced so that it will hang horizontally.

ODETTE

••

B Cloud 001

| 1 | 2 | 2 | 2 | 2 | 2 | x50gm |

(Also shown in Angel 002 and Cloud 001)

NEEDLES
1 pair 4mm (no 8) (US 6) needles
1 pair 4½mm (no 7) (US 7) needles
4mm (no 8) (US 6) circular needle

BUTTONS – 4 x 00318 or 00401

TENSION
20 sts and 28 rows to 10 cm measured over stocking stitch using 4½mm (US 7) needles.

BACK
Using 4mm (US 6) needles and yarn B cast on 52 [58: 62: 64: 68: 70] sts.
Work in g st for 2 rows, ending with RS facing for next row.
Change to 4½mm (US 7) needles and A.
Beg and ending rows as indicated, using the **fairisle** technique as described on the information page and repeating the 20 row patt repeat throughout, cont in patt from chart for body, which is worked entirely in st st, as folls:
Cont straight until back meas 17 [19: 22: 23: 25: 26] cm, ending with RS facing for next row.
Shape armholes
Keeping patt correct, cast off 3 sts at beg of next 2 rows. 46 [52: 56: 58: 62: 64] sts.
Dec 1 st at each end of next and foll 2 alt rows. 40 [46: 50: 52: 56: 58] sts.
Cont straight until armhole meas 11 [12: 13: 14: 14: 15] cm, ending with RS facing for next row.
Shape shoulders
Cast off 4 [5: 6: 6: 7: 7] sts at beg of next 2 rows, then 5 [6: 6: 7: 7: 8] sts at beg of foll 2 rows.
Break yarn and leave rem 22 [24: 26: 26: 28: 28] sts on a holder.

LEFT FRONT
Using 4mm (US 6) needles and yarn B cast on 38 [41: 45: 46: 50: 51] sts.

Work in g st for 2 rows, ending with RS facing for next row.
Change to 4½mm (US 7) needles and A.
Beg and ending rows as indicated, cont in patt from chart for body until left front matches back to beg of armhole shaping, ending with RS facing for next row.
Shape armhole
Keeping patt correct, cast off 3 sts at beg of next row. 35 [38: 42: 43: 47: 48] sts.
Work 1 row.
Dec 1 st at armhole edge of next and foll 2 alt rows.
32 [35: 39: 40: 44: 45] sts.
Cont straight until left front matches back to beg of shoulder shaping, ending with RS facing for next row.
Shape shoulder
Cast off 4 [5: 6: 6: 7: 7] sts at beg of next row, then 5 [6: 6: 7: 7: 8] sts at beg of foll alt row.
Work 1 row, ending with RS facing for next row.
Break yarn and leave rem 23 [24: 27: 27: 30: 30] sts on a holder.

RIGHT FRONT
Work as given for left front, reversing shapings.

SLEEVES
Using 4mm (US 6) needles and yarn B cast on 34 [36: 38: 40: 40: 42] sts.
Work in g st for 2 rows, ending with RS facing for next row.
Change to 4½mm (US 7) needles and A.
Beg with a K row, work in st st, shaping sides by dec 1 st at each end of 5th [5th: next: 3rd: next: next] and foll 0 [0: 6th: 6th: 6th: 6th] row. 32 [34: 34: 36: 36: 38] sts.
Work 4 [4: 4: 2: 4: 4] rows, ending with **WS** of cuff (RS of main sleeve) facing for next row.
Beg and ending rows as indicated, using the **fairisle** technique as described on the information page and repeating the 20 row patt repeat throughout, cont in patt from chart for sleeve, which is worked entirely in st st beg with a K row, as folls:

Inc 1 st at each end of 5th [5th: 5th: 3rd: 5th: 5th] and every foll 6th row to 40 [42: 52: 56: 52: 54] sts, then on every foll 8th [8th: –: –: : 8th: 8th] row until there are 44 [48: –: –: 56: 60] sts.
Cont straight until sleeve meas 17 [20: 23: 25: 27: 30] cm **from beg of chart**, ending with RS facing for next row.
Shape top
Keeping patt correct, cast off 3 sts at beg of next 2 rows.
38 [42: 46: 50: 50: 54] sts.
Dec 1 st at each end of next and foll alt row, then on foll row, ending with RS facing for next row.
Cast off rem 32 [36: 40: 44: 44: 48] sts.

MAKING UP
Press as described on the information page.
Join both shoulder seams using back stitch, or mattress stitch if preferred.
Hood
With RS facing, using 4½mm (US 7) needles and appropriate yarn(s) at set by patt on back and fronts, beg and ending at front opening edges, patt 23 [24: 27: 27: 30: 30] sts of right front, 22 [24: 26: 26: 28: 28] sts of back, then 23 [24: 27: 27: 30: 30] sts of left front.
68 [72: 80: 80: 88: 88] sts.
Place marker between centre 2 sts.
Keeping patt correct as set by back and fronts, cont as folls:
Work 1 row.
Row 2 (RS): Patt to within 1 st of marker, M1, patt 2 sts (marker is between these sts), M1, patt to end.
Work 1 row.
Row 4: As row 2.
Work 3 rows.
Row 8: As row 2.
74 [78: 86: 86: 94: 94] sts.
Cont straight until hood meas 17 [18: 19: 20: 21: 22] cm from pick-up row, ending with RS facing for next row.
Cast off.
Following chart, swiss darn vertical lines onto all pieces.
Join top (cast-off edge) seam of hood.

YARN

	3-6	6-12				
			1-2	2-3	3-4	4-5	months
							years

To fit chest

| 46 | 51 | 56 | 58 | 61 | 64 | cm |
| 18 | 20 | 22 | 23 | 24 | 25 | in |

Rowan Soft Baby

A Princess 003

| 2 | 3 | 3 | 4 | 4 | 4 | x50gm |

Front and hood edging

With RS facing, using 4mm (US 6) circular needle and yarn B, beg and ending at cast-on edges, pick up and knit 56 [62: 70: 74: 78: 82] sts up right front opening edge to hood pick-up row, 34 [36: 38: 40: 42: 44] sts up right side of hood to top seam, 34 [36: 38: 40: 42: 44] sts down left side of hood to hood pick-up row, then 56 [62: 70: 74: 78: 82] sts down left front opening edge.

180 [196: 216: 228: 240: 252] sts.

Work in g st for 2 rows, ending with **WS** facing for next row.

Cast off knitwise (on WS).

See information page for finishing instructions, setting in sleeves using the shallow set-in method and reversing sleeve seam for contrast turn-back cuff. Fold cuff to RS.

Make 3 button loops along one front opening edge (right front for a girl, or left front for a boy), placing top button loop level with beg of armhole shaping and rem 2 button loops spaced 5 [5: 6: 6: 7. 7] cm apart below top loop. Attach buttons to RS of other front to correspond with button loops. Make 1 button loop along other front opening edge level with beg of armhole shaping and attach button to inside of other front to correspond with this button loop.

Make 5 cm long tassel using B and attach to point of hood.

Body chart

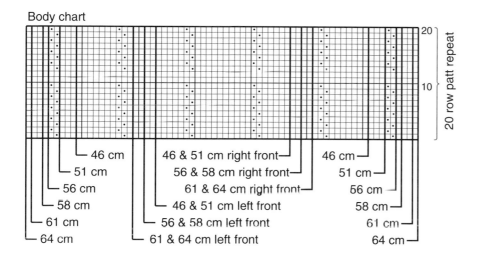

Sleeve chart

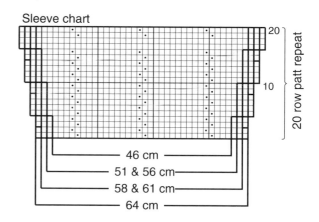

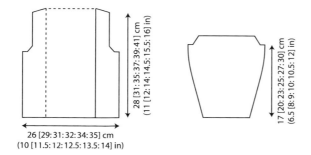

26 [29: 31: 32: 34: 35] cm
(10 [11.5: 12: 12.5: 13.5: 14] in)

28 [31: 35: 37: 39: 41] cm
(11 [12: 14: 14.5: 15.5: 16] in)

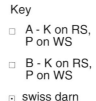

17 [20: 23: 25: 27: 30] cm
(6.5 [8: 9: 10: 10.5: 12] in)

Key

☐ A - K on RS, P on WS

☐ B - K on RS, P on WS

⊡ swiss darn using B

AGNES

•

YARN

						months
3-6	6-12					
		1-2	2-3	3-4	4-5	years

To fit chest

46	51	56	58	61	64	cm
18	20	22	23	24	25	in

Rowan Soft Baby

A Cloud 001

2	3	3	3	4	4	x 50gm

B Princess 003

1	1	1	1	1	1	x 50gm

Oddment of Rowan 4 ply Soft in contrast colour (Raincloud 387) for legs
Oddment of Rowan Soft Baby in contrast colour (Buttercup 008) for beak

NEEDLES

1 pair 4mm (no 8) (US 6) needles
1 pair 4½mm (no 7) (US 7) needles
3.25mm (no 10) (US D3) crochet hook
4.00mm (no 8) (US G6) crochet hook

BUTTONS – 3 x 00318 and 2 x 00333 (for chick eyes)

TENSION

20 sts and 28 rows to 10 cm measured over stocking stitch using 4½mm (US 7) needles and yarn A.

CROCHET ABBREVIATIONS

ch = chain; **ss** = slip stitch; **dc** = double crochet.

BACK

Using 4mm (US 6) needles and yarn A cast on 50 [58: 62: 62: 66: 70] sts.

Row 1 (RS): K2, *P2, K2, rep from * to end.
Row 2: P2, *K2, P2, rep from * to end.
These 2 rows form rib.
Work in rib for a further 4 [4: 6: 6: 6: 6] rows, inc [dec: dec: inc: inc: dec] 1 st at end of last row and ending with RS facing for next row.
51 [57: 61: 63: 67: 69] sts.
Change to 4½mm (US 7) needles.
Beg with a K row, work in st st until back meas 15 [17: 20: 21: 23: 25] cm, ending with RS facing for next row.
Shape raglan armholes
Cast off 3 sts at beg of next 2 rows.
45 [51: 55: 57: 61: 63] sts.**
Next row (RS): K1, sl 1, K1, psso, K to last 3 sts, K2tog, K1.
Working all raglan armhole decreases as set by last row, dec 1 st at each end of 4th and every foll 4th row to 33 [41: 43: 45: 51: 55] sts, then on every foll alt row until 21 [23: 25: 25: 27: 27] sts rem.
Work 1 row, ending with RS facing for next row.
Cast off.

FRONT

Work as given for Back to **.
Working all raglan armhole decreases as set by back, dec 1 st at each end of next and every foll 4th row until 39 [45: 49: 49: 53: 55] sts rem.
Work 0 [2: 2: 0: 0: 0] rows, ending with **WS** facing for next row.
Next row (WS): P to last st, K1.
This row sets the sts – left raglan edge st worked as a K st on every row and all other sts still in st st.
Keeping raglan decreases and sts correct as set, work 2 rows, dec 0 [1: 1: 0: 0: 1] st at each end of first of these rows and ending with RS facing for next row. 39 [43: 47: 49: 53: 53] sts.
Next row (RS): (K first st and slip this st back onto left needle) 5 times (to make a button loop), K first st again, (sl 1, K1, psso) 1 [0: 0: 1: 1: 1] times, K to last 3 [0: 0: 3: 3: 3] sts, (K2tog, K1) 1 [0: 0: 1: 1: 1] times.
37 [43: 47: 47: 51: 51] sts.

Making another button loop on foll 10th [10th: 12th: 12th: 12th: 12th] row (and noting that no further reference will be made to button loop), dec 1 st at each end of 4th [2nd: 2nd: 4th: 2nd: 2nd] and foll 0 [alt: 4th: alt: alt: alt] row, then on foll 0 [0: 0: 0: 1: 1] alt rows.
35 [39: 43: 43: 45: 45] sts.
Work 1 row, ending with RS facing for next row.
Shape neck
Next row (RS): (K1, sl 1, K1, psso) 0 [1: 1: 1: 1: 1] times, K14 [12: 14: 14: 14: 14] and turn, leaving rem sts on a holder.
Work each side of neck separately.
Dec 1 st at neck edge of next 4 rows, then on foll 2 [2: 3: 3: 3: 3] alt rows **and at same time** dec 1 st at raglan armhole edge on 2nd and every foll alt row. 4 sts.
Work 1 row, ending with RS facing for next row.
Next row (RS): K1, sl 1, K2tog, psso.
Next row: P1, K1.
Next row: K2tog and fasten off.
With RS facing, rejoin yarn to rem sts, cast off centre 7 [9: 9: 9: 11: 11] sts, K to last 0 [3: 3: 3: 3: 3] sts, (K2tog, K1) 0 [1: 1: 1: 1: 1] times.
Complete to match first side, reversing shapings.

LEFT SLEEVE

Using 4mm (US 6) needles and yarn A cast on 30 [34: 34: 34: 34: 38] sts.
Work in rib as given for back for 6 rows, inc 1 [0: 0: 1: 1: 0] st at each end of last row and ending with RS facing for next row.
32 [34: 34: 36: 36: 38] sts.
Change to 4½mm (US 7) needles.
Beg with a K row, work in st st, shaping sides by inc 1 st at each end of 5th [7th: 5th: 5th: 5th: 7th] and every foll 6th [8th: 6th: 6th: 6th: 8th] row to 38 [44: 50: 48: 42: 42] sts, then on every foll 8th [-: -: 8th: 8th: 10th] row until there are 42 [-: -: 52: 52: 52] sts.
Cont straight until sleeve meas 17 [20: 23: 25: 27: 30] cm, ending with RS facing for next row.

Shape raglan
Cast off 3 sts at beg of next 2 rows. 36 [38: 44: 46: 46: 46] sts.***
Working all raglan decreases as set by back, dec 1 st at each end of next and every foll 4th row to 32 [32: 40: 42: 42: 42] sts, then on foll 0 [0: 2: 3: 3: 3] alt rows. 32 [32: 36: 36: 36: 36] sts.
Work 2 [0: 0: 0: 0: 0] rows, ending with **WS** facing for next row.
Next row (WS): Cast on and K 2 sts, P to end. 34 [34: 38: 38: 38: 38] sts.
Next row: K1, sl 1, K1, psso, K to last 5 sts, K2tog, K3.
Next row: K2, P to end.
Last 2 rows set the sts – front raglan edge 2 sts in g st with all other sts still in st st.
Working all decreases as set by last 2 rows and keeping sts correct, dec 1 st at each end of next and every foll alt row until 10 sts rem, ending with **WS** facing for next row.
Cast off 5 sts at beg of next row. 5 sts.
Next row (RS): K1, sl 1, K1, psso, K2tog. 3 sts.
Next row: P2tog, P1.
Next row (RS): K2tog and fasten off.

RIGHT SLEEVE

Work as given for left sleeve to ***.
Working all raglan decreases as set by back, dec 1 st at each end of next and every foll 4th row to 30 [32: 40: 42: 42: 42] sts, then on every foll alt row until 10 sts rem.
Work 1 row, ending with RS facing for next row.
Cast off 3 sts at beg and dec 1 st at end of next row. 6 sts.
Dec 1 st at end of next row. 5 sts.
Next row (RS): (K2tog) twice, K1. 3 sts.
Next row: P1, P2tog.
Next row (RS): K2tog and fasten off.

MAKING UP

Press as described on the information page.
Leaving left front raglan open for last 22 [22: 26: 26: 26: 26] rows (for buttoned opening), join raglan seams using back stitch, or mattress stitch if preferred. Sew 2 cast-on sts at base of left raglan opening in place on inside.

Neckband

With RS facing, using 4mm (US 6) needles and yarn A, beg and ending at left front raglan opening edges, pick up and knit 12 [12: 13: 13: 13: 13] sts down left side of neck, 7 [9: 9: 9: 11: 11] sts from front, 12 [12: 13: 13: 13: 13] sts up right side of neck, 6 sts from right sleeve, 20 [22: 24: 24: 26: 26] sts from back, then 8 sts from left sleeve.
65 [69: 73: 73: 77: 77] sts.
Row 1 (WS): *K2, P2, rep from * to last st, K1.
Row 2: K3, *P2, K2, rep from * to last 2 sts, K2.
These 2 rows set the sts.
Cont as set for a further 4 rows, making a button loop as before at beg of 2nd of these rows and ending with **WS** facing for next row.
Cast off in patt.

See information page for finishing instructions.
Chick body
Using yarn B, work as given for front and back of Agnes toy to end of round 5.
Fasten off.
Wings (make 2)
Using yarn B, work as given for wings of Agnes toy to end of row 2.
Fasten off.
Using photograph as a guide, sew chick onto front of sweater. Sew wings to each side of body, with straight edges of wings against body and leaving curved edges free to "flap". Using yellow yarn, embroider 3 straight stitches for beak as in photograph. Sew on 2 small buttons for eyes.
Legs (both alike)
Using 3.25mm (US D3) crochet hook and oddment of 4 ply Soft, make 11 ch, ss into

6th ch from hook, 7 ch, ss into same ch as before, 5 ch, ss into same ch as before.
Fasten off.

Using photograph as a guide, sew straight length of 5 ch of each leg in place to base of body.

25.5 [28.5: 30.5: 31.5: 33.5: 34.5] cm
(10 [11: 12: 12.5: 13: 13.5] in)

28 [31: 35: 37: 39: 41] cm
(11 [12: 14: 14.5: 15.5: 16] in)

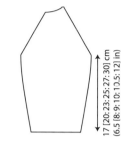

17 [20: 23: 25: 27: 30] cm
(6.5 [8: 9: 10: 10.5: 12] in)

HANNAH HAT

YARN

	3-6	6-12				months
			1-2	2-3	3-4	4-5 years

To fit chest

| 46 | 51 | 56 | 58 | 61 | 64 | cm |
| 18 | 20 | 22 | 23 | 24 | 25 | in |

Rowan Soft Baby and Kidsilk Haze

A Baby Cosy 004						
1	1	1	2	2	2	x 50gm

B BabyPrin.003						
1	1	1	1	1	1	x 50gm

Oddments of Kidsilk Haze in 3 contrast colours (C – Majestic 589, D – Dewberry 600, and E – Grace 580) for flowers and embroidery

NEEDLES

1 pair 4mm (no 8) (US 6) needles
1 pair 4½mm (no 7) (US 7) needles
2.50 [2.50: 3.00: 3.00: 3.50: 3.50]mm (no 12 [12: 11: 11: 9: 9]) (US C2 [C2: D3: D3: E4: E4]) crochet hook

TENSION
20 sts and 28 rows to 10 cm measured over stocking stitch using 4½mm (US 7) needles and yarn A.

CROCHET ABBREVIATIONS
ss = slip stitch; **ch** = chain; **dc** = double crochet; **htr** = half treble; **tr** = treble; **dtr** = double treble; **sp(s)** = space(s).

HAT (worked from top downwards)
Using 4½mm (US 7) needles and yarn A cast on 67 [73: 79: 85: 91: 97] sts.
Beg with a K row, work in st st for 14 [15: 16: 17: 18: 19] cm, ending with **WS** facing for next row.
Beg again with a K row (to reverse RS of work), work in st st for a further 4 cm, ending after a K row.
Change to 4mm (US 6) needles.
Break off yarn A and join in yarn B.

Work in g st for 3 rows, ending with RS facing for next row.
Work picot cast-off as folls: cast off 2 sts, *slip st on right needle back onto left needle, cast on 2 sts, cast off 4 sts, rep from * until all sts are cast off.

MAKING UP
Press as described on the information page. Join back seam using back stitch, or mattress stitch if preferred, reversing seam for last 5 cm. Fold hat flat, with seam running centrally along tube, and join cast-on edges to form top seam.
Using yarn A, make two 6 cm tassels and attach one to each end of top seam.
Make one large, one medium and one small flower as given for Hannah sweater. Using photograph as a guide, sew flowers onto front of hat. Using yarn C DOUBLE and chain st, embroider stems and leaves as in photograph.

BEA

• • •

YARN

	3-6	6-12					months
			1-2	2-3	3-4	4-5	years
To fit chest							
	46	51	56	58	61	64	cm
	18	20	22	23	24	25	in

Rowan Soft Baby

| 3 | 3 | 3 | 4 | 4 | 5 | x50gm |

(photographed in Cloud 001)

NEEDLES

1 pair 4mm (no 8) (US 6) needles
1 pair 4½mm (no 7) (US 7) needles
Cable needle

BUTTONS – 3 x 00318

TENSION

20 sts and 28 rows to 10 cm measured over
stocking stitch using 4½mm (US 7) needles.

SPECIAL ABBREVIATIONS

wyaf = with yarn at front (WS) of work;
wyab = with yarn at back (RS) of work;
C2B = slip next st onto cable needle and
leave at back of work, K1, then K1 from cable
needle; **C2F** = slip next st onto cable needle
and leave at front of work, K1, then K1 from
cable needle; **Cr2R** = slip next st onto cable
needle and leave at back of work, K1, then P1
from cable needle; **Cr2L** = slip next st onto
cable needle and leave at front of work, P1,
then K1 from cable needle.

BACK

Using 4mm (US 6) needles cast on 81 [87:
93: 95: 99: 101] sts.
Row 1 (RS): K1, *P1, K1, rep from * to end.
Row 2: As row 1.
These 2 rows form moss st.
Work in moss st for a further 3 [3: 5: 5: 5: 5]
rows, ending with **WS** facing for next row.
Change to 4½mm (US 7) needles.
Row 1 (WS): P28 [31: 34: 35: 37: 38],
sl 1 wyaf, P5, sl 1 wyab, P11, sl 1 wyab, P5,
sl 1 wyaf, P to end.
Row 2: Knit.
These 2 rows form patt.
Cont in patt, shaping side seams by dec 1 st at
each end of 8th and every foll 14th [18th:
14th: 16th: 18th: 18th] row until 75 [81: 85:
87: 91: 93] sts rem.
Cont straight until back meas 19 [22: 25: 27:
30: 31] cm, ending with **WS** facing for
next row.
Next row (WS): P26 [29: 31: 32: 34: 35],
cast off next 23 sts purlwise, P to end.
52 [58: 62: 64: 68: 70] sts.
Work in g st for 2 rows.
Beg with a K row, work in st st for 2 rows.
Work in g st for 2 rows, ending with RS
facing for next row.
Beg and ending rows as indicated and
repeating the 8 row patt repeat throughout,
cont in patt from chart as folls:
Work 2 rows, ending with RS facing for
next row.
Shape armholes
Keeping patt correct, cast off 3 sts at beg of
next 2 rows.
46 [52: 56: 58: 62: 64] sts.
Dec 1 st at each end of next 3 rows, then on
foll 1 [2: 2: 2: 2: 2] alt rows.
38 [42: 46: 48: 52: 54] sts.
Cont straight until armhole meas 11 [12: 13:
14: 14: 15] cm, ending with RS facing for
next row.

Shape shoulders and back neck
Next row (RS): Cast off 4 [4: 5: 5: 6: 6] sts,
patt until there are 7 [8: 8: 9: 9: 10] sts on
right needle and turn, leaving rem sts on
a holder.
Work each side of neck separately.
Cast off 3 sts at beg of next row.
Cast off rem 4 [5: 5: 6: 6: 7] sts.
With RS facing, rejoin yarn to rem sts,
cast off centre 16 [18: 20: 20: 22: 22] sts,
patt to end.
Complete to match first side, reversing
shapings.

LEFT FRONT

Using 4mm (US 6) needles cast on 32 [35:
38: 39: 41: 42] sts.
Row 1 (RS): *K1, P1, rep from * to last
0 [1: 0: 1: 1: 0] st, K0 [1: 0: 1: 1: 0].
Row 2: K0 [1: 0: 1: 1: 0], *P1, K1, rep from *
to end.
These 2 rows form moss st.
Work in moss st for a further 2 [2: 4: 4: 4: 4]
rows, ending with RS facing for next row.
Next row (RS): Moss st to last 5 sts and
turn, leaving rem 5 sts on a holder.
27 [30: 33: 34: 36: 37] sts.
Change to 4½mm (US 7) needles.
Beg with a P row, work in st st, shaping side
seams by dec 1 st at beg of 10th and every
foll 14th [18th: 14th: 16th: 18th: 18th] row
until 24 [27: 29: 30: 32: 33] sts rem.
Cont straight until left front meas 19 [22: 25:
27: 30: 31] cm, ending with RS facing for
next row.
Work in g st for 2 rows.
Beg with a K row, work in st st for 2 rows.
Work in g st for 2 rows, ending with RS
facing for next row.
Beg and ending rows as indicated, cont in
patt from chart as folls:
Work 2 rows, ending with RS facing for next
row. (Left front should now match back to
beg of armhole shaping.)
Shape armhole
Keeping patt correct, cast off 3 sts at beg of
next row.
21 [24: 26: 27: 29: 30] sts.

Work 1 row.
Dec 1 st at armhole edge of next 3 rows, then
on foll 1 [2: 2: 2: 2: 2] alt rows.
17 [19: 21: 22: 24: 25] sts.
Cont straight until 13 [13: 15: 15: 15: 15]
rows less have been worked than on back to
beg of shoulder shaping, ending with **WS**
facing for next row.
Shape neck
Keeping patt correct, cast off 2 [3: 3: 3: 4: 4]
sts at beg of next row.
15 [16: 18: 19: 20: 21] sts.
Dec 1 st at neck edge on next 5 rows, then
on foll 2 [2: 3: 3: 3: 3] alt rows.
8 [9: 10: 11: 12: 13] sts.
Work 3 rows, ending with RS facing for
next row.
Shape shoulder
Cast off 4 [4: 5: 5: 6: 6] sts at beg of next row.
Work 1 row.
Cast off rem 4 [5: 5: 6: 6: 7] sts.

RIGHT FRONT

Using 4mm (US 6) needles cast on 32 [35:
38: 39: 41: 42] sts.
Row 1 (RS): K0 [1: 0: 1: 1: 0], *P1, K1, rep
from * to end.
Row 2: *K1, P1, rep from * to last 0 [1: 0: 1:
1: 0] st, K0 [1: 0: 1: 1: 0].
These 2 rows form moss st.
Work in moss st for a further 2 [2: 4: 4: 4: 4]
rows, ending with RS facing for next row.
Next row (RS): Moss st 5 sts and slip these
sts onto a holder, moss st to end.
27 [30: 33: 34: 36: 37] sts.
Change to 4½mm (US 7) needles.
Beg with a P row, work in st st, shaping side
seams by dec 1 st at end of 10th and every
foll 14th [18th: 14th: 16th: 18th: 18th] row
until 24 [27: 29: 30: 32: 33] sts rem.
Complete to match left front, reversing shapings.

SLEEVES

Using 4mm (US 6) needles cast on 31 [33:
33: 35: 35: 37] sts.
Work in moss st as given for back for 5 [5: 5:
7: 7: 7] rows, ending with **WS** facing for
next row.

Change to 4½mm (US 7) needles.
Beg with a P row, work in st st, shaping sides by inc 1 st at each end of 6th [6th: 2nd: 2nd: 2nd: 2nd] and every foll 14th [12th: 10th: 10th: 10th: 10th] row to 37 [41: 39: 45: 43: 49] sts, then on every foll - [-: 12th: 8th: 12th: 12th] row until there are - [-: 43: 47: 47: 51] sts.
Cont straight until sleeve meas 17 [20: 23: 25: 27: 30] cm, ending with RS facing for next row.

Shape top
Cast off 3 sts at beg of next 2 rows.
31 [35: 37: 41: 41: 45] sts.
Dec 1 st at each end of next 3 rows, then on foll 6 [6: 7: 7: 7: 7] alt rows, then on foll 1 [3: 3: 5: 5: 7] rows, ending with RS facing for next row.
Cast off rem 11 sts.

MAKING UP
Press as described on the information page. Join both shoulder seams using back stitch, or mattress stitch if preferred.

Button border
Slip 5 sts from left front holder onto 4mm (US 6) needles and rejoin yarn with RS facing.
Cont in moss st as set until border, when slightly stretched, fits up left front opening edge to neck shaping, ending with RS facing for next row.
Cast off.
Slip st border in place.
Mark positions for 3 buttons on this border – first to come between the 2 g st ridges at underarm, last to come 1.5 cm below neck shaping, and rem button evenly spaced between.

Buttonhole border
Slip 5 sts from right front holder onto 4mm (US 6) needles and rejoin yarn with **WS** facing.
Cont in moss st as set until border, when slightly stretched, fits up right front opening edge to neck shaping, ending with RS facing for next row and with the addition of 3 buttonholes to correspond with positions marked for buttons worked as folls:
Buttonhole row (RS): Moss st 1 st, work 2 tog, yrn, moss st 2 sts.
When border is complete, cast off.
Slip st border in place.

Collar
Using 4mm (US 6) needles cast on 67 [73: 79: 79: 85: 85] sts.
Work in moss st as given for back for 3 [3: 4: 4: 5: 5] cm, ending with RS facing for next row.
Dec 1 st at each end of next and foll alt row, then on foll 3 rows, ending with RS facing

for next row.
57 [63: 69: 69: 75: 75] sts.
Break yarn.
With RS facing and using 4mm (US 6) needles, pick up and knit 13 [13: 15: 15: 17: 17] sts along row-end edge from cast-on edge to sts on needle, K 57 [63: 69: 69: 75: 75] sts on needle, then pick up and knit 13 [13: 15: 15: 17: 17] sts along other row-end edge to cast-on edge.
83 [89: 99: 99: 109: 109] sts.

Cast off loosely knitwise (on WS).
Sew cast-on edge of collar to neck edge, easing in slight fullness and positioning cast-off edge of collar edging halfway across top of borders.
Form pleat in back below yoke by folding along slip st lines and sewing cast-off edge in place on inside.
See information page for finishing instructions, setting in sleeves using the set-in method.

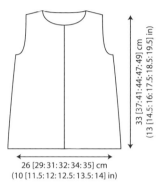

33 [37: 41: 44: 47: 49] cm
(13 [14.5: 16: 17.5: 18.5: 19.5] in)

26 [29: 31: 32: 34: 35] cm
(10 [11.5: 12: 12.5: 13.5: 14] in)

17 [20: 23: 25: 27: 30] cm
(6.5 [8: 9: 10: 10.5: 12] in)

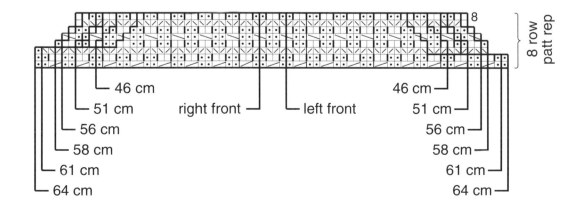

8
8 row patt rep

46 cm
51 cm
56 cm
58 cm
61 cm
64 cm

right front

left front

46 cm
51 cm
56 cm
58 cm
61 cm
64 cm

Key

☐ K on RS, P on WS

▫ P on RS, K on WS

◹ C2B

◺ C2F

Cr2R

Cr2L

AGNES MOBILE & PRAM STRING

••

YARN
Rowan Soft Baby
Mobile
A Princess 003   1 x 50gm
B Cloud 001   1 x 50gm
Oddment of Rowan 4 ply Soft in contrast colour (387) for legs
Oddment of Rowan Soft Baby in contrast colour (007) for beak
Pram string
A Princess 003   1 x 50gm
B Cloud 001   1 x 50gm

Oddment of Rowan 4 ply Soft in contrast colour (387) for legs
Oddment of Rowan Soft Baby in contrast colour (007) for beaks

CROCHET HOOKS
3.25mm (no 10) (US D3) crochet hook
4.00mm (no 8) (US G6) crochet hook

EXTRAS – Mobile and pram string:
Washable toy filling. **Mobile:** Wooden (or metal) ring 46 cm (18 ins) in diameter, 6 m of 4 cm (1½ in) wide ribbon, 3.60 m of narrow ribbon and metal curtain ring.16 x 00333 buttons for eyes **Pram string**: 2 metres of 0.8 cm wide ribbon. 10 x 00333 buttons for eyes

FINISHED SIZE
Completed smaller chicks are approx 10 cm (4 ins) tall, and larger chicks are approx 12 cm (4½ ins) tall, both excluding legs.

TENSION
14 sts and 17 rows to 10 cm measured over double crochet fabric using 4.00mm (US G6) hook.

CROCHET ABBREVIATIONS
ch = chain; **ss** = slip stitch; **dc** = double crochet.

Mobile

SMALLER CHICKS (make 4)
Front and back (both alike)
Using yarn A, work as given for front and back of Agnes toy to end of round 4.
Fasten off.
Wings (make 2)
Using yarn A, work as given for wings of Agnes toy to end of row 2.
Fasten off.

LARGER CHICKS (make 4)
Front and back (both alike)
Using yarn B, work as given for front and back of Agnes toy to end of round 6.
Fasten off.
Wings (make 2)
Using yarn B, work as given for wings of Agnes toy to end of row 2.
Fasten off.

MAKING UP
Press as described on the information page. Sew back and front of each chick together, leaving an opening to insert toy filling. Insert toy filling and close opening. Sew straight ends of wings to sides of chick.
Using photograph as a guide and yellow yarn, embroider 3 straight stitches for beak. Sew on 2 small buttons for eyes.
Legs (both alike)
Using 3.25mm (US D3) crochet hook and oddment of 4 ply Soft, make 11 ch, ss into 6th ch from hook, 7 ch, ss into same ch as before, 5 ch, ss into same ch as before, 1 dc into each of next 5 ch and fasten off.
Attach ends of legs to lower edge of chick as in photograph.
Wrap length of ribbon around wooden ring so that it is completely covered and secure in place. From narrow ribbon, cut four 90 cm lengths for hanging strips. Join centres of hanging strips and attach curtain ring at this point. Attach ends of these ribbons to wooden ring at eight evenly spaced points around ring. Using 4.00 mm (US G6) crochet hook and same colour yarn as each chick, make 8 lengths of chain of varying lengths and attach one to each chick. Attach other end to wooden ring directly below hanging strips – alternate size of chicks attached to ring and vary lengths of chain, ensuring mobile is balanced so that it will hang horizontally.

Pram string

SMALLER CHICKS (make 4)
Front and back (both alike)
Using yarn A, work as given for front and back of Agnes toy to end of round 4.
Fasten off.
Wings (make 2)
Using yarn A, work as given for wings of Agnes toy to end of row 2.
Fasten off.

LARGER CHICK
Front and back (both alike)
Using yarn B, work as given for front and back of Agnes toy to end of round 6.
Fasten off.
Wings (make 2)
Using yarn B, work as given for wings of Agnes toy to end of row 2.
Fasten off.

MAKING UP
Press as described on the information page. Sew back and front of each chick together, leaving an opening to insert toy filling. Insert toy filling and close opening. Sew straight ends of wings to sides of chick.
Using photograph as a guide and yellow yarn, embroider 3 straight stitches for beak. Sew on 2 small buttons for eyes.
Legs (both alike)
Using 3.25mm (US D3) crochet hook and oddment of 4 ply Soft, make 11 ch, ss into 6th ch from hook, 7 ch, ss into same ch as before, 5 ch, ss into same ch as before, 1 dc into each of next 5 ch and fasten off.
Attach ends of legs to lower edge of chick as in photograph.
Attach larger chick to centre of length of ribbon, then 2 smaller chicks either side of this larger chick, placing chicks approx 8 cm apart. Tie ends of ribbon to sides of pram.

JASPER TOY

YARN
Rowan Soft Baby
    1   x 50gm
(photographed in 002)

NEEDLES
1 pair 4mm (no 8) (US 6) needles

EXTRAS
EXTRAS – Oddments of Rowan 4 ply Soft in contrast colour (387) for mouth, and Soft Baby in 2nd contrast colour (003) for tongue, 3 buttons for eyes, and washable toy filling

FINISHED SIZE
Completed toy is approx 14 cm (5½ins) tall.

TENSION
Based on a stocking stitch tension of 20 sts and 28 rows to 10 cm using 4½mm (US 7) needles.

FRONT
Left arm
Using 4mm (US 6) needles cast on 5 sts.
Row 1 (WS): Purl.
Row 2: Inc in first st, K to last st, inc in last st. 7 sts.
Row 3: Inc in first st, P to end. 8 sts.

Row 4: K to last st, inc in last st. 9 sts.
Row 5: Inc in first st, P to last 2 sts, P2tog.
Row 6: K2tog, K to last st, inc in last st.
Break yarn and leave rem 9 sts on a holder.
Left leg
Using 4mm (US 6) needles cast on 9 sts.
Row 1 (RS): Knit.
Row 2: Inc in first st, P to last st, inc in last st. 11 sts.
Row 3: Inc in first st, K to last st, inc in last st. 13 sts.
Row 4: Purl.
Row 5: K2tog, K to last st, inc in last st.
Break yarn and leave rem 13 sts on a holder.
Right leg
Using 4mm (US 6) needles cast on 10 sts.
Row 1 (RS): Knit.
Row 2: Inc in first st, P to last st, inc in last st. 12 sts.
Row 3: Inc in first st, K to end. 13 sts.
Row 4: Purl.
Row 5: Inc in first st, K to last st, K2tog.
Join legs
Row 6 (WS): Work across sts of right leg as folls: P2tog, P to last st, inc in last st, now with WS facing work across sts of left leg as folls: inc in first st, P to last 2 sts, P2tog. 26 sts.
Row 7: K2tog, K to last 2 sts, K2tog. 24 sts.
Row 8: P to last 2 sts, P2tog. 23 sts.
Row 9: K2tog, K to end. 22 sts.
Row 10: As row 8. 21 sts.
Row 11: Knit.
Row 12: As row 8. 20 sts.
Row 13: Knit.
Break yarn and leave rem 20 sts on a holder.

Right arm
Using 4mm (US 6) needles cast on 7 sts.
Row 1 (WS): Purl.
Row 2: Inc in first st, K to last st, inc in last st. 9 sts.
Row 3: P to last st, inc in last st. 10 sts.
Row 4: Inc in first st, K to end. 11 sts.
Row 5: P2tog, P to last st, inc in last st.
Row 6: Inc in first st, K to last 2 sts, K2tog.
Row 7: Cast off 4 sts, P to last st, inc in last st. 8 sts.
Row 8: As row 6.
Join right arm to body
Row 14 (of body) (WS): Work across sts of right arm as folls: cast off 2 sts, P to last st, inc in last st, now with WS facing work across sts of body as folls: P20. 27 sts.
Row 15: K2tog, K to last 2 sts, K2tog.
Join left arm to body
Row 16 (WS): Work across sts of body as folls: P25, turn and cast on 4 sts, turn and now with WS facing work across sts of left arm as folls: P to last 2 sts, P2tog. 37 sts.
Row 17: Cast off 2 sts, K to last 2 sts, K2tog. 34 sts.
Row 18: P2tog, P to last 2 sts, P2tog. 32 sts.
Row 19: Cast off 3 sts, K to last 2 sts, K2tog. 28 sts.
Row 20: As row 18. 26 sts.
Row 21: Cast off 3 sts, K to end. 23 sts.
Row 22: Purl.
Row 23: Knit.
Row 24: P to last st, inc in last st. 24 sts.
Row 25: Inc in first st, K to last st, inc in last st. 26 sts.
Row 26: Inc in first st, P to end. 27 sts.

Row 27: Inc in first st, K to end. 28 sts.
Row 28: As row 26. 29 sts.
Row 29: Knit.
Row 30: Inc in first st, P to last st, inc in last st. 31 sts.
Row 31: Knit.
Row 32: Purl.
Row 33: Knit.
Row 34: P2tog, P to last 2 sts, P2tog. 29 sts.
Row 35: K to last 2 sts, K2tog. 28 sts.
Row 36: P to last 2 sts, P2tog. 27 sts.
Row 37: K2tog, K to last 2 sts, K2tog. 25 sts.
Row 38: P2tog, P to last 2 sts, P2tog. 23 sts.
Row 39: Cast off 3 sts, K to last 2 sts, K2tog. 19 sts.
Row 40: Cast off 3 sts, P to last 2 sts, P2tog. Cast off rem 15 sts.

BACK
Work as given for front, but reading K for P and P for K (and reading WS for RS and vice versa) to reverse shape of knitted piece.

MAKING UP
Press as described on the information page. Using oddments of contrast yarns and photograph as a guide, embroider mouth onto front in stem st, then tongue in fly stitch. Sew front and back together around entire outer edge, leaving an opening to insert toy filling. Insert toy filling, then close opening.
Securely attach button eyes as in photograph.

ALEXIS

• • •

YARN

3-6	6-12					months
		1-2	2-3	3-4	4-5	years
To fit chest						
46	51	56	58	61	64	cm
18	20	22	23	24	25	in

Rowan Soft Baby and 4 ply Soft

A SoftCosy 004

| 2 | 2 | 2 | 3 | 3 | 3 | x 50gm |

B *4 plyLins.393

| 2 | 2 | 3 | 3 | 3 | 4 | x 50gm |

C Soft Cloud 001

| 1 | 1 | 1 | 2 | 2 | x 50gm |

D *4 ply Folly 391

| 2 | 2 | 3 | 3 | 3 | 3 | x 50gm |

*Use 4 ply Soft DOUBLE throughout (also shown in Soft Baby 003, 004 and 4 ply Soft 378 and 386)

NEEDLES

1 pair 4mm (no 8) (US 6) needles
1 pair 4½mm (no 7) (US 7) needles
4mm (no 8) (US 6) circular needle

BUTTONS – 3 x 00348

TENSION

21 sts and 32 rows to 10 cm measured over pattern using 4½mm (US 7) needles.

Pattern note: Whilst working patt, slip all sts purlwise with yarn at **wrong side** of work.

BACK

Using 4mm (US 6) needles and yarn A cast on 57 [61: 67: 69: 73: 75] sts.
Row 1 (RS): K1, *P1, K1, rep from * to end.
Row 2: P1, *K1, P1, rep from * to end.
These 2 rows form rib.
Work in rib for a further 3 [3: 5: 5: 5: 5] rows, ending with **WS** facing for next row.
Next row (WS): Rib 4 [2: 1: 2: 4: 1], rib next st winding yarn 3 times round needle, *rib 3, rib next st winding yarn 3 times round needle, rep from * to last 4 [2: 1: 2: 4: 1] sts, rib to end.
Change to 4½mm (US 7) needles.
Joining in colours as required, cont in patt as folls:
Row 1 (RS): Using yarn B, K4 [2: 1: 2: 4: 1], sl next st dropping extra loops, *K3, sl next st dropping extra loops, rep from * to last 4 [2: 1: 2: 4: 1] sts, K to end.
Row 2: Using yarn B, P4 [2: 1: 2: 4: 1], sl 1, *P3, sl 1, rep from * to last 4 [2: 1: 2: 4: 1] sts, P to end.
Row 3: Using yarn B, K4 [2: 1: 2: 4: 1], sl 1, *K3, sl 1, rep from * to last 4 [2: 1: 2: 4: 1] sts, K to end.

Row 4: Using yarn B, P4 [2: 1: 2: 4: 1], P next st winding yarn 3 times round needle, *P3, P next st winding yarn 3 times round needle, rep from * to last 4 [2: 1: 2: 4: 1] sts, P to end.
Rows 5 to 8: Using yarn C, as rows 1 to 4.
Rows 9 to 12: Using yarn D, as rows 1 to 4.
Rows 13 to 16: Using yarn A, as rows 1 to 4.
These 16 rows form patt.
Cont in patt until back meas 23 [26: 29: 31: 34: 35] cm, ending with RS facing for next row.
Shape armholes
Keeping patt correct, cast off 2 sts at beg of next 2 rows.
53 [57: 63: 65: 69: 71] sts.
Dec 1 st at each end of next 4 rows.
45 [49: 55: 57: 61: 63] sts.
Cont straight until armhole meas 11 [12: 13: 14: 14: 15] cm, ending with RS facing for next row.
Shape shoulders and back neck
Next row (RS): Cast off 5 [6: 7: 7: 8: 8] sts, patt until there are 9 [9: 10: 11: 11: 12] sts on right needle and turn, leaving rem sts on a holder.
Work each side of neck separately.
Cast off 3 sts at beg of next row.
Cast off rem 6 [6: 7: 8: 8: 9] sts.
With RS facing, rejoin yarns to rem sts, cast off centre 17 [19: 21: 21: 23: 23] sts, patt to end.
Complete to match first side, reversing shapings.

POCKET LININGS (make 2)
Using 4 1/2mm (US 7) needles and yarn C [D: D: A: B: C] cast on 15 [15: 17: 17: 19: 19] sts.
Beg with a K row, work in st st for 15 [15: 17: 17: 19: 19] rows, inc 1 st at each end of last row and ending with **WS** facing for next row. 17 [17: 19: 19: 21: 21] sts.
Next row (WS): P2 [2: 1: 1: 2: 2], P next st winding yarn 3 times round needle, *P3, P next st winding yarn 3 times round needle, rep from * to last 2 [2: 1: 1: 2: 2] sts, P to end.
Break yarn and leave sts on a holder.

LEFT FRONT
Using 4mm (US 6) needles and yarn A cast on 28 [30: 32: 34: 36: 36] sts.
Row 1 (RS): *K1, P1, rep from * to last 2 sts, K2.
Row 2: *K1, P1, rep from * to end.
These 2 rows form rib.
Work in rib for a further 3 [3: 5: 5: 5: 5] rows, ending with **WS** facing for next row.
Next row (WS): (Work 2 tog) 1 [1: 0: 1: 1: 0] times, rib 1 [1: 2: 1: 1: 2], *rib next st winding yarn 3 times round needle, rib 3, rep from * to last 5 [3: 2: 3: 5: 2] sts, rib next st winding yarn 3 times round needle, rib 4 [2: 1: 2: 4: 1]. 27 [29: 32: 33: 35: 36] sts.
Change to 4½mm (US 7) needles.
Joining in colours as required, cont in patt as folls:
Row 1 (RS): Using yarn B, K4 [2: 1: 2: 4: 1], sl next st dropping extra loops, *K3, sl next st dropping extra loops, rep from * to last 2 sts, K2.
Row 2: Using yarn B, P2, sl 1, *P3, sl 1, rep from * to last 4 [2: 1: 2: 4: 1] sts, P to end.
Row 3: Using yarn B, K4 [2: 1: 2: 4: 1], sl 1, *K3, sl 1, rep from * to last 2 sts, K2.
Row 4: Using yarn B, P2, P next st winding yarn 3 times round needle, *P3, P next st winding yarn 3 times round needle, rep from * to last 4 [2: 1: 2: 4: 1] sts, P to end.
Rows 5 to 8: Using yarn C, as rows 1 to 4.
Rows 9 to 12: Using yarn D, as rows 1 to 4.
Rows 13 to 16: Using yarn A, as rows 1 to 4.
These 16 rows form patt.
Work in patt for a further 7 [11: 11: 15: 19: 23] rows, ending after patt row 7 [11: 11: 15: 3: 7] and with **WS** facing for next row.
Next row (WS): Using same yarn as previous row, patt 4 [4: 5: 5: 8: 8] sts, P17 [17: 19: 19: 21: 21], patt to end.
Place pocket
Next row (RS): Patt 6 [8: 8: 9: 6: 7] sts, slip next 17 [17: 19: 19: 21: 21] sts onto a holder and, in their place, patt across 17 [17: 19: 19: 21: 21] sts of first pocket lining, patt to end.
Cont straight until left front matches back to beg of armhole shaping, ending with RS facing for next row.
Shape armhole

Keeping patt correct, cast off 2 sts at beg of next row. 25 [27: 30: 31: 33: 34] sts.
Work 1 row.
Dec 1 st at armhole edge of next 4 rows. 21 [23: 26: 27: 29: 30] sts.
Cont straight until 13 [13: 15: 15: 15: 15] rows less have been worked than on back to beg of shoulder shaping, ending with **WS** facing for next row.
Shape neck
Keeping patt correct, cast off 3 [4: 4: 4: 5: 5] sts at beg of next row. 18 [19: 22: 23: 24: 25] sts.
Dec 1 st at neck edge of next 5 rows, then on foll 2 [2: 3: 3: 3: 3] alt rows. 11 [12: 14: 15: 16: 17] sts.
Work 3 rows, ending with RS facing for next row.
Shape shoulder
Cast off 5 [6: 7: 7: 8: 8] sts at beg of next row.
Work 1 row.
Cast off rem 6 [6: 7: 8: 8: 9] sts.

RIGHT FRONT
Using 4mm (US 6) needles and yarn A cast on 28 [30: 32: 34: 36: 36] sts.
Row 1 (RS): K2, *P1, K1, rep from * to end.
Row 2: *P1, K1, rep from * to end.
These 2 rows form rib.
Work in rib for a further 3 [3: 5: 5: 5: 5] rows, ending with **WS** facing for next row.
Next row (WS): Rib 4 [2: 1: 2: 4: 1], rib next st winding yarn 3 times round needle, *rib 3, rib next st winding yarn 3 times round needle, rep from * to last 3 [3: 2: 3: 3: 2] sts, rib 1 [1: 2: 1: 1: 2], (work 2 tog) 1 [1: 0: 1: 1: 0] times. 27 [29: 32: 33: 35: 36] sts.
Change to 4½mm (US 7) needles.
Joining in colours as required, cont in patt as folls:
Row 1 (RS): Using yarn B, K2, sl next st dropping extra loops, *K3, sl next st dropping extra loops, rep from * to last 4 [2: 1: 2: 4: 1] sts, K to end.
Row 2: Using yarn B, P4 [2: 1: 2: 4: 1], sl 1, *P3, sl 1, rep from * to last 2 sts, P2.
Row 3: Using yarn B, K2, sl 1, *K3, sl 1, rep from * to last 4 [2: 1: 2: 4: 1] sts, K to end.
Row 4: Using yarn B, P4 [2: 1: 2: 4: 1], P next st winding yarn 3 times round needle, *P3, P next st winding yarn 3 times round needle, rep from * to last 2 sts, P2.
Rows 5 to 8: Using yarn C, as rows 1 to 4.
Rows 9 to 12: Using yarn D, as rows 1 to 4.
Rows 13 to 16: Using yarn A, as rows 1 to 4.

These 16 rows form patt.
Work in patt for a further 7 [11: 11: 15: 19: 23] rows, ending after patt row 7 [11: 11: 15: 3: 7] and with **WS** facing for next row.
Next row (WS): Using same yarn as previous row, patt 6 [8: 8: 9: 6: 7] sts, P17 [17: 19: 19: 21: 21], patt to end.
Place pocket
Next row (RS): Patt 4 [4: 5: 5: 8: 8] sts, slip next 17 [17: 19: 19: 21: 21] sts onto a holder and, in their place, patt across 17 [17: 19: 19: 21: 21] sts of second pocket lining, patt to end.
Complete to match left front, reversing shapings.

SLEEVES
Using 4mm (US 6) needles and yarn A cast on 33 [35: 35: 37: 37: 39] sts.
Work in rib given for back for 5 [5: 7: 7: 7: 7] rows, ending with **WS** facing for next row.
Next row (WS): Rib 2 [3: 3: 2: 2: 1], rib next st winding yarn 3 times round needle, *rib 3, rib next st winding yarn 3 times round needle, rep from * to last 2 [3: 3: 2: 2: 1] sts, rib to end.
Change to 4½mm (US 7) needles.
Joining in colours as required, cont in patt as folls:
Row 1 (RS): Using yarn B, K2 [3: 3: 2: 2: 1], sl next st dropping extra loops, *K3, sl next st dropping extra loops, rep from * to last 2 [3: 3: 2: 2: 1] sts, K to end.
Row 2: Using yarn B, P2 [3: 3: 2: 2: 1], sl 1, *P3, sl 1, rep from * to last 2 [3: 3: 2: 2: 1] sts, P to end.
Row 3: Using yarn B, K2 [3: 3: 2: 2: 1], sl 1, *K3, sl 1, rep from * to last 2 [3: 3: 2: 2: 1] sts, K to end.
Row 4: Using yarn B, P2 [3: 3: 2: 2: 1], P next st winding yarn 3 times round needle, *P3, P next st winding yarn 3 times round needle, rep from * to last 2 [3: 3: 2: 2: 1] sts, P to end.
These 4 rows set position of patt as given for back.
Cont in patt, shaping sides by inc 1 st at each end of next [3rd: next: next: 3rd: 3rd] and every foll 4th [6th: 4th: 4th: 6th: 6th] row to 37 [51: 43: 43: 59: 59] sts, then on every foll 6th [-: 6th: 6th: -: 8th] row until there are 47 [-: 55: 59: -: 63] sts, taking inc sts into patt.
Cont straight until sleeve meas approx 17 [20: 23: 25: 27: 30] cm, ending after patt row 2, 6, 10 or 14 and with RS facing for next row.

Shape top
Keeping patt correct, cast off 2 sts at beg of next 2 rows. 43 [47: 51: 55: 55: 59] sts.
Dec 1 st at each end of next 3 rows, ending with **WS** facing for next row.
Next row (WS): Using same yarn as previous row, P2tog, P to last 2 sts, P2tog.
Cast off rem 35 [39: 43: 47: 47: 51] sts.

MAKING UP
Press as described on the information page.
Join both shoulder seams using back stitch, or mattress stitch if preferred.

Hood
With RS facing, using 4½mm (US 7) needles and yarn A, beg and ending at front opening edges, pick up and knit 14 [16: 19: 19: 21: 21] sts up right side of neck, 22 [25: 25: 26: 26: 29] sts from back, then 14 [16: 19: 19: 21: 21] sts down left side of neck. 50 [57: 64: 64: 71: 71] sts.
Next row (WS): P2, *P next st winding yarn 3 times round needle, inc purlwise in next st, P1, P next st winding yarn 3 times round needle, P3, rep from * to last 6 sts, P next st winding yarn 3 times round needle, inc purlwise in next st, P1, P next st winding yarn 3 times round needle, P2. 57 [65: 73: 73: 81: 81] sts.
Joining in colours as required, cont in patt as folls:
Row 1 (RS): Using yarn B, K2, sl next st dropping extra loops, *K3, sl next st dropping extra loops, rep from * to last 2 sts, K2.

Row 2: Using yarn B, P2, *sl 1, P3, rep from * to last 3 sts, sl 1, P2.
Row 3: Using yarn B, K2, *sl 1, K3, rep from * to last 3 sts, sl 1, K2.
Row 4: Using yarn B, P2, *P next st winding yarn 3 times round needle, P3, rep from * to last 3 sts, P next st winding yarn 3 times round needle, P2.
These 4 rows set position of patt as given for back.
Cont in patt as set until hood meas approx 18 [19: 20: 20: 21: 21] cm from pick-up row, ending after patt row 4, 8, 12 or 16 and with RS facing for next row.
Shape top
Place marker on centre st of last row.
Row 1 (RS): Patt to within 2 sts of marked st, K2tog, patt marked st, K2tog tbl, patt to end.
Work 1 row.
Rep last 2 rows once more. 53 [61: 69: 69: 77: 77] sts.
Row 5 (RS): Patt to within 2 sts of marked st, K2tog, patt marked st, K2tog tbl, patt to end.
Row 6: Patt to within 2 sts of marked st, P2tog tbl, patt marked st, P2tog, patt to end.
Row 7: As row 5. 47 [55: 63: 63: 71: 71] sts.
Row 8: Using same yarn as previous row, P to within 2 sts of marked st, P2tog tbl, P marked st, P2tog, P to end.
Cast off rem 45 [53: 61: 61: 69: 69] sts.
Join top (cast-off) seam of hood.
Front and hood border
With RS facing, using 4mm (US 6) circular needle and yarn A, beg and ending at cast-on

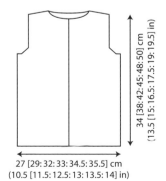

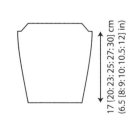

34 [38: 42: 45: 48: 50] cm
(13.5 [15: 16.5: 17.5: 19: 19.5] in)

27 [29: 32: 33: 34.5: 35.5] cm
(10.5 [11.5: 12.5: 13: 13.5: 14] in)

17 [20: 23: 25: 27: 30] cm
(6.5 [8: 9: 10: 10.5: 12] in)

edges, pick up and knit 60 [68: 75: 81: 87: 91] sts up right front opening edge to hood pickup row, 81 [87: 91: 91: 95: 95] sts from front edge of hood to hood pick-up row, then 60 [68: 75: 81: 87: 91] sts down left front opening edge.
201 [223: 241: 253: 269: 277] sts.

Row 1 (WS): K1, *P1, K1, rep from * to end.
Row 2: K2, *P1, K1, rep from * to last st, K1.
These 2 rows form rib.
Work in rib for a further 4 rows, ending with **WS** facing for next row.
Cast off in rib (on **WS**).

Pocket tops (both alike)
Slip 17 [17: 19: 19: 21: 21] sts from pocket holder onto 4mm (US 6) needles and rejoin yarn A with RS facing.
Beg with row 2, work in rib as given for front and hood border for 6 rows, ending with RS facing for next row.

Cast off in rib.
See information page for finishing instructions, setting in sleeves using the shallow set-in method. Using yarn B, make 3 twisted or crochet cords, each 7 cm long, and attach to fronts as in photograph to form button loops.

BRUNO

● ●

YARN

	3-12			months
		1-3	3-5	years
Rowan Soft Baby				
	1	1	1	x 50gm

(photographed in Angel 002)

NEEDLES
1 pair 4mm (no 8) (US 6) needles
1 pair 4½mm (no 7) (US 7) needles

BUTTONS – 1 x (00392) and 1 x (00387)

TENSION
20 sts and 28 rows to 10 cm measured over stocking stitch using 4½mm (US 7) needles.

CROWN
Using 4½mm (US 7) needles cast on 74 [83: 92] sts.
Beg with a K row, work in st st for 8 [9: 10] cm, ending with RS facing for next row.
Shape top
Row 1 (RS): K1, (K2tog, K5, K2tog tbl) 8 [9: 10] times, K1.
58 [65: 72] sts.
Work 3 rows.
Row 5: K1, (K2tog, K3, K2tog tbl) 8 [9: 10] times, K1. 42 [47: 52] sts.
Work 3 rows.
Row 9: K1, (K2tog, K1, K2tog tbl) 8 [9: 10] times, K1. 26 [29: 32] sts.
Work 3 rows.
Row 13: K1, (sl 1, K2tog, psso) 8 [9: 10] times, K1. 10 [11: 12] sts.
Row 14: P0 [1: 0], (P2tog) 5 [5: 6] times.
Break yarn and thread through rem 5 [6: 6] sts. Pull up tight and fasten off securely.

BACK FLAP
Using 4mm (US 6) needles cast on
53 [59: 65] sts.

Row 1 (RS): K1, *P1, K1, rep from * to end.
Row 2: As row 1.
These 2 rows form moss st.
Work in moss st for a further 6 [8: 10] rows, ending with RS facing for next row.
Dec 1 st at each end of next and foll 2 alt rows, then on foll 4 rows, ending with **WS** facing for next row.
39 [45: 51] sts.
Break yarn.
With **WS** facing and using 4mm (US 6) needles, pick up and knit 19 [21: 23] sts up first side of flap from cast-on edge to sts on needle, moss st across 39 [45: 51] sts on needle, then pick up and knit 19 [21: 23] sts down second side of flap to cast-on edge.
77 [87: 97] sts.
Beg with a K row, work in st st for 4 rows.
Cast off loosely.

FRONT FLAP
Using 4mm (US 6) needles cast on
21 [23: 27] sts.
Work in moss st as given for back flap for 8 [10: 12] rows, ending with RS facing for next row.
Dec 1 st at each end of next and foll 2 alt rows, then on foll 2 rows, ending with **WS**

facing for next row. 11 [13: 17] sts.
Break yarn.
With **WS** facing and using 4mm (US 6) needles, pick up and knit 17 [19: 21] sts up first side of flap from cast-on edge to sts on needle, moss st across 11 [13: 17] sts on needle, then pick up and knit 17 [19: 21] sts down second side of flap to cast-on edge.
45 [51: 59] sts.
Beg with a K row, work in st st for 4 rows.
Cast off loosely.

MAKING UP
Press as described on the information page. Join back seam using back stitch, or mattress stitch if preferred. Mark points along cast-on edge of crown 13.5 [15: 16.5] cm either side of back seam. Using photograph as a guide and allowing last few rows of st st of back flap to roll over (to cover pick-up row), sew cast-on edge of back flap to cast-on edge of back section of crown between markers, matching pick-up row of st st edging to markers. In same way, sew cast-on edge of front flap to rem free cast-on section of crown so that row-end edges of flaps meet and rolled st st sections overlap. Sew buttons to top of crown, placing smaller button on top of larger button.

HANNAH SCARF

Rowan Soft Baby and Kidsilk Haze
A BabyCosy004

| 1 | 1 | 1 | 2 | 2 | 2 | x 50gm |

B BabyPrin.003

| 1 | 1 | 1 | 1 | 1 | 1 | x 50gm |

Oddments of Kidsilk Haze in 3 contrast colours (C – Majestic 589, D – Pebbles 572, and E – Grace 580) for flowers and embroidery

NEEDLES
1 pair 4mm (no 8) (US 6) needles
1 pair 4½mm (no 7) (US 7) needles
2.50 [2.50: 3.00: 3.00: 3.50: 3.50]mm (no 12 [12: 11: 11: 9: 9]) (US C2 [C2: D3: D3: E4: E4]) crochet hook

YARN

3-6	6-12					months
		1-2	2-3	3-4	4-5	years
To fit chest						
46	51	56	58	61	64	cm
18	20	22	23	24	25	in

FINISHED SIZE
Completed scarf measures 10 [11: 12: 13: 14: 15] cm (4 [4½: 4½: 5: 5½: 6] in) wide and 86 [91: 96: 101: 106: 111] cm (34 [36: 38: 40: 41½: 43½] in) long.

TENSION
20 sts and 28 rows to 10 cm measured over stocking stitch using 4½mm (US 7) needles and yarn A.

CROCHET ABBREVIATIONS
ss = slip stitch; **ch** = chain; **dc** = double crochet; **htr** = half treble; **tr** = treble; **dtr** = double treble; **sp(s)** = space(s).

SCARF
Using 4½mm (US 7) needles and yarn A cast on 20 [22: 24: 26: 28: 30] sts.
Row 1 (RS): Knit.
Row 2: K1, P to last st, K1.
Rep these 2 rows until scarf meas 80 [85: 90: 95: 100: 105] cm, ending with RS facing for next row.
Cast off.

MAKING UP
Press as described on the information page.

Edging
Using 4mm (US 6) needles and yarn B cast on 5 sts.
Row 1 (RS): K3, (yfwd) twice, K2.
Row 2: K2, K into front and back of double yfwd of previous row, K3. 7 sts.
Row 3: K7.
Row 4: Cast off 2 sts, K to end. 5 sts.
These 4 rows form patt.
Cont in patt until edging fits across cast-on edge of scarf, ending after patt row 4.
Cast off.
Slip stitch straight edge in place to cast-on edge.
In same way, make and attach edging to cast-off edge.
Make 2 large, 2 medium and 2 small flowers as given for Hannah sweater. Using photograph as a guide, sew flowers onto ends of scarf. Using yarn C DOUBLE and chain st, embroider stems and leaves as in photograph.

STOCKIST INFORMATION
ROWAN OVERSEAS DISTRIBUTORS

AUSTRALIA:
Australian Country Spinners
314 Albert Street
Brunswick
Victoria 3056
Tel: (03) 9380 3888
Email: sales@auspinners.com.au

BELGIUM:
Pavan
Meerlaanstraat 73
B9860 Balegem (Oosterzele)
Tel: (32) 9 221 8594
Email: pavan@pandora.be

CANADA:
Diamond Yarn
9697 St Laurent, Montreal
Quebec, H3L 2N1
Tel: (514) 388 6188

Diamond Yarn (Toronto),
155 Martin Ross, Unit 3
Toronto
Ontario, M3J 2L9
Tel: (416) 736 6111
Email: diamond@diamondyarn.com
www.diamondyarns.com

DENMARK
Individual stockists please contact
Rowan for details

FRANCE:
Elle Tricot
8 Rue du Coq
67000 Strasbourg
Tel: (33) 3 88 23 03 13
Email: elletricot@agat.net
www.elletricote.com

GERMANY:
Wolle & Design
Wolfshovener Strasse 76
52428 Julich-Stetternich
Tel: (49) 2461 54735
Email: Info@wolleunddesign.de
www.wolleunddesign.de

Coats GMbH
Eduardstrasse 44
D-73084 Salach
Tel: (49) 7162 / 14-346
www.coatsgmbh.de

HOLLAND:
de Afstap
Oude Leliestraat 12
1015 AW Amsterdam
Tel: (31) 20 6231445

HONG KONG:
East Unity Co Ltd
Unit B2, 7/F Block B
Kailey Industrial Centre
12 Fung Yip Street, Chai Wan
Tel: (852) 2869 7110
Fax: (852) 2537 6952
Email: eastuni@netvigator.com

ICELAND:
Storkurinn
Laugavegi 59
101 Reykjavik
Tel: (354) 551 8258
Fax: (354) 562 8252
Email: malin@mmedia.is

ITALY:
D.L. srl
Via Piave, 24 – 26, 20016 Pero
Milan
Tel: (39) 02 339 10 180.

FINLAND:
Oy Nordia Produkter Ab
Mikkolantie 1
00640 Helsinki
Tel: (358) 9 777 4272
Email: info@nordiaprodukter.fi

JAPAN:
Puppy Co Ltd
T151-0051
3-16-5 Sendagaya
Shibuyaku, Tokyo
Tel: (81) 3 3490 2827
Email: info@rowan-jaeger.com

KOREA:
Coats Korea Co Ltd
5F Kuckdong B/D
935-40 Bangbae- Dong
Seocho-Gu, Seoul
Tel: (82) 2 521 6262
Fax: (82) 2 521 5181

NEW ZEALAND
Individual stockists please contact
Rowan for details

NORWAY:
Coats Norge A/S
Postboks 63, 2801 Gjovik
Tel: (47) 61 18 34 00
Fax: (47) 61 18 34 20

SINGAPORE:
Golden Dragon Store
101 Upper Cross Street #02-51
People's Park Centre
Singapore 058357
Tel: (65) 6 5358454
Email: gdscraft@hotmail.com

SOUTH AFRICA:
Arthur Bales PTY
PO Box 44644
Linden 2104
Tel: (27) 11 888 2401

SPAIN:
Oyambre
Pau Claris 145, 80009 Barcelona
Tel: (34) 670 011957
Email: comercial@oyambreonline.com

SWEDEN:
Wincent
Norrtullsgatan 65, 113 45 Stockholm
Tel: (46) 8 33 70 60
Fax: (46) 8 33 70 68
Email: wincent@chello.se
www.wincentyarn.com

TAIWAN :
Laiter Wool Knitting Co Ltd
10-1 313 Lane, Sec 3
Chung Ching North Road
Taipei
Tel: (886) 2 2596 0269

Long T eh Trading Co Ltd
3F No. 19-2
Kung Yuan Road, Taichung
Tel: (886) 4 2225 6698

Green Leave Thread Company
No 181
Sec 4 Chung Ching North Road
Taipei
Fax: (886) 2 8221 2919

U.S.A.:
Westminster Fibers Inc
4 Townsend West
Suite 8, Nashua
New Hampshire 03063
Tel: (1 603) 886 5041 / 5043
Email: rowan@westminsterfibers.com

U.K.:
Rowan Yarns
Green Lane Mill, Holmfirth
West Yorkshire, HD9 2DX.
Tel : 01484 681881
Email: littletreasures@knitrowan.com.
www.knitrowan.com

**For all other countries:
please contact Rowan for
stockist details.**

For details of U.K. stockists or any
other information concerning this
brochure please contact:
Rowan Yarns, Green Lane Mill,
Holmfirth, West Yorkshire,
England, HD9 2DX
Email: littletreasures@knitrowan.com
Internet: www.knitrowan.com

TENSION

Obtaining the correct tension is perhaps the single factor which can make the difference between a successful garment and a disastrous one. It controls both the shape and size of an article, so any variation, however slight, can distort the finished garment.

Different designers feature in our books and it is **their** tension, given at the **start** of each pattern, which you must match. We recommend that you knit a square in pattern and/or stocking stitch (depending on the pattern instructions) of perhaps 5 - 10 more stitches and 5 - 10 more rows than those given in the tension note. Mark out the central 10cm square with pins. If you have too many stitches to 10cm try again using thicker needles, if you have too few stitches to 10cm try again using finer needles. Once you have achieved the correct tension your garment will be knitted to the measurements indicated in the size diagram shown at the end of the pattern.

SIZING & SIZE DIAGRAM NOTE

The instructions are given for the smallest size. Where they vary, work the figures in brackets for the larger sizes. **One set of figures refers to all sizes.** Included with most patterns in this brochure is a 'size diagram', or sketch of the finished garment and its dimensions. The size diagram shows the finished width of the garment at the under-arm point, and it is this measurement that the knitter should choose first; a useful tip is to measure one of your own garments which is a comfortable fit. Having chosen a size based on width, look at the corresponding length for that size; if you are not happy with the total length which we recommend, adjust your own garment before beginning your armhole shaping - any adjustment after this point will mean that

your sleeve will not fit into your garment easily - don't forget to take your adjustment into account if there is any side seam shaping. Finally, look at the sleeve length; the size diagram shows the finished sleeve measurement, taking into account any top-arm insertion length. Measure your body between the centre of your neck and your wrist, this measurement should correspond to half the garment width plus the sleeve length. Again, your sleeve length may be adjusted, but remember to take into consideration your sleeve increases if you do adjust the length - you must increase more frequently than the pattern states to shorten your sleeve, less frequently to lengthen it.

CHART NOTE

Many of the patterns in the brochure are worked from charts. Each square on a chart represents a stitch and each line of squares a row of knitting. Each colour used is given a different letter and these are shown in the **materials** section, or in the **key** alongside the chart of each pattern. When working from the charts, read odd rows (K) from right to left and even rows (P) from left to right, unless otherwise stated.

KNITTING WITH COLOUR

There are two main methods of working colour into a knitted fabric: **Intarsia** and **Fairisle** techniques. The first method produces a single thickness of fabric and is usually used where a colour is only required in a particular area of a row and does not form a repeating pattern across the row, as in the fairisle technique.

Intarsia: The simplest way to do this is to cut short lengths of yarn for each motif or block of colour used in a row. Then joining in the various colours at the appropriate point on the row, link one colour to the next by

twisting them around each other where they meet on the wrong side to avoid gaps. All ends can then either be darned along the colour join lines, as each motif is completed or then can be " knitted in" to the fabric of the knitting as each colour is worked into the pattern. This is done in much the same way as "weaving- in" yarns when working the Fairisle technique and does save time darning-in ends. It is essential that the tension is noted for **Intarsia** as this may vary from the stocking stitch if both are used in the same pattern.

Fairisle type knitting: When two or three colours are worked repeatedly across a row, strand the yarn **not** in use loosely behind the stitches being worked. If you are working with more than two colours, treat the "floating" yarns as if they were one yarn and always spread the stitches to their correct width to keep them elastic. It is advisable not to carry the stranded or "floating" yarns over more than three stitches at a time, but to weave them under and over the colour you are working. The "floating" yarns are therefore caught at the back of the work.

CROCHET TERMS

UK crochet terms and abbreviations have been used throughout. The list below gives the US equivalent where they vary.

Abbreviation UK		US
dc	double crochet	single crochet
tr	treble	double crochet
htr	half treble	half double crochet
dtr	double treble	treble

FINISHING INSTRUCTIONS

After working for hours knitting a garment, it seems a great pity that many garments are spoiled because such little care is taken in the pressing and finishing process. Follow the following tips for a truly professional-looking garment.

PRESSING

Block out each piece of knitting and following the instructions on the ball band press the garment pieces, omitting the ribs. Tip: Take special care to press the edges, as this will make sewing up both easier and neater. If the ball band indicates that the fabric is not to be pressed, then covering the blocked out fabric with a damp white cotton cloth and leaving it to stand will have the desired effect. Darn in all ends neatly along the selvage edge or a colour join, as appropriate.

STITCHING

When stitching the pieces together, remember to match areas of colour and texture very carefully where they meet. Use a seam stitch such as back stitch or mattress stitch for all main knitting seams and join all ribs and neckband with mattress stitch, unless otherwise stated.

CONSTRUCTION

Having completed the pattern instructions, join left shoulder and neckband seams as detailed above. Sew the top of the sleeve to the body of the garment using the method detailed in the pattern, referring to the appropriate guide:

Shallow set-in sleeves: Match decreases at beg of armhole shaping to decreases at top of sleeve. Sew sleeve head into armhole, easing in shapings.

Set- in sleeves: Place centre of cast-off edge of sleeve to shoulder seam. Set in sleeve, easing sleeve head into armhole.

Join side and sleeve seams.
Slip stitch pocket edgings and linings into place. Sew on buttons to correspond with buttonholes.
Ribbed welts and neckbands and any areas of garter stitch should not be pressed.

ABBREVIATIONS

K	knit	**rep**	repeat	**tbl**	through back of loop
P	purl	**alt**	alternate	**yrn**	yarn round needle
st(s)	stitch(es)	**cont**	continue	**yfwd**	yarn forward
inc	increas(e)(ing)	**patt**	pattern	**meas**	measures
dec	decreas(e)(ing)	**tog**	together	**0**	no stitches, times or rows
st st	stocking stitch (1 row K, 1 row P)	**mm**	millimetres	**–**	no stitches, times or rows for
g st	garter stitch (K every row)	**cm**	centimetres		that size
beg	begin(ning)	**in(s)**	inch(es)	**approx**	approximately
foll	following	**RS**	right side		
rem	remain(ing)	**WS**	wrong side		
rev st st	reverse stocking stitch (1 row P, 1 row K)	**sl 1**	slip one stitch		
		psso	pass slipped stitch over		

Chain Stitch

Fly Stitch

Satin Stitch

Stem Stitch

EXPERIENCE RATINGS

●   Easy, straight forward knitting / crocheting

● ●   Suitable for the average knitter / crocheter

● ● ●   For the more experienced knitter

Photographer Gisela Torres • Stylist Marina Olivati • Hair & Make-up Jeni Dodson • Models Aliyah Daniels, Blewes Rush, Kara Laurent,
Lola Tustain, Amaranta Chavez, Isla Holley, Jerry St Hilaire, Charlie Coleman, Harrison Coleman, Rupert Cullinane, Cameron Meola
Design Layout Simon Wagstaff

First published in Great Britain in 2005 by Rowan Yarns Ltd, Green Lane Mill, Holmfirth, West Yorkshire, England, HD9 2DX
Internet: www.knitrowan.com Email: littletreasures@knitrowan.com
© Copyright Rowan 2005
British Library Cataloguing in Publication Data Rowan Yarns - Little Treasures
ISBN 1-904485-49-9